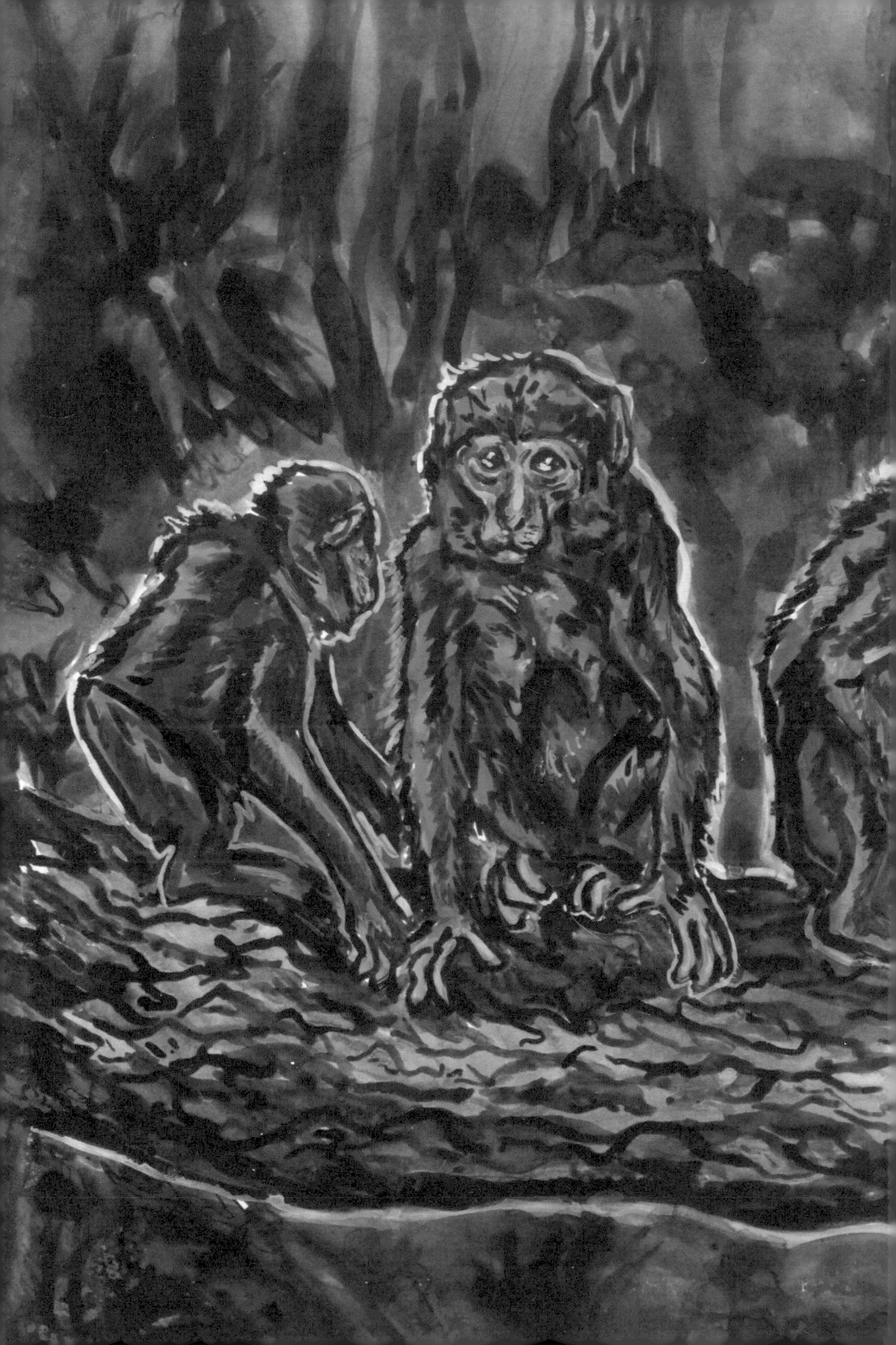

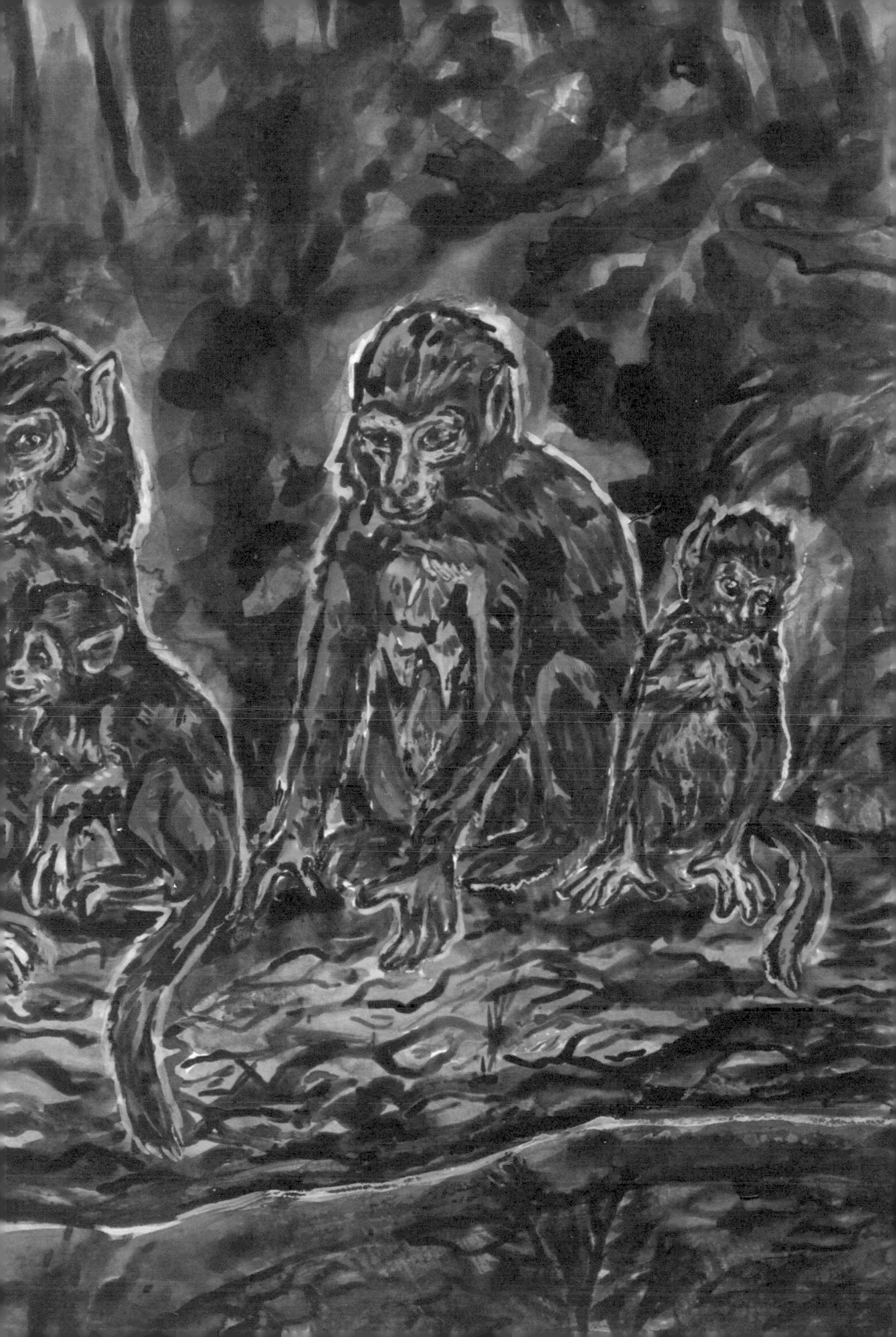

Praise for *SALT*

"Wow, this is a true out-of-left field masterpiece from a cartoonist I hadn't heard of before seeing this work. Intense and pouring over with color and a rich narrative, this is truly a unique experience of a book. Jacobs is working from a world of imagery all his own and the experience of reading this is a singular one. Don't sleep on this."—**Austin English**, cartoonist and artist, Owner of Domino Books: Mind-expanding comics for freethinkers.

"*SALT* brings movement to the movement, utilizing the graphic novel medium as a hopeful method of reimagining historical fiction. Drawn with expressive urgency, Jacobs illustrates the heartbreak, responsibility, and fears that can coincide with animal rescue activism. Our protagonist's mental state trails into nightmarish moments that expose the challenge of practicing an ethics of care in a world that normalizes violence."
—**Suzy González**, visual artist

"To see Jacobs's art is to be challenged into a deeper sensitivity; drawn in by the densely packed, kaleidoscoping waterfalls and explosions of hope and pain that saturate each page in its own technicolor nightmare-vs-dream landscape. Brushstrokes capture the expressions of humans and other-than-humans against shifting backdrops dotted by minimalist utterances that require you to draw upon your most raw emotions and join in a collective yearning for any sign of compassion. *SALT* reveals a world that is at the same time hopeless and hopeful—that merges identities of human and non-human animals into both the heroes and the victims—within a journey that gives no guarantee of safe passage. I feel like Jacobs's art is unto itself a form of essential, beautiful, heartbreaking, and unsparing activism. Animal rights activists live balancing impossible realities and Jacobs's art is the language of that experience."—**Rebecca Moore**, Founder and Executive Director, The Institute for Animal Happiness

"Touching. Unsettling. Soul-stirring. I'm in awe of Jacobs's art! *SALT* tells the story of three wounded spirits crossing paths towards healing. Poignant images, meaningful dialogues and a powerful preface combine to awaken us from our collective cultural insanity. SALT reminds us that nonviolence is the only thing that will make us feel whole again." —**Dr. Camila Perussello**, author of *Food for Thought: Planetary Healing Begins on Our Plate*

"In his allegorical comic, Jacobs reveals the relational and psychic dimensions of trauma, anxiety, and care in the context of animal exploitation in scientific research and the activists who intervene. Deftly using raw, colorful illustration and relatable dialog, Jacob illustrates, through fiction, the lived reality by those who take risks to save animals from their systems of oppression."—**Linnea Ryshke**, author of *Kindling: Poetry and Art*

SALT

A confessional animal liberation narrative

Coyote Jacobs

Lantern Publishing & Media • Woodstock & Brooklyn, NY

2023
Lantern Publishing & Media
PO Box 1350
Woodstock, NY 12498
www.lanternpm.org

Printed in the United States of America

Library of Congress Cataloging-in-Publication Data

Names: Jacobs, Coyote, author, artist. | Waltz-Rieber, Charles, writer of foreword.
Title: Salt : a confessional animal liberation narrative / Coyote Jacobs ; foreword by Charles Waltz-Rieber.
Description: Woodstock : Lantern Publishing & Media, 2023.
Identifiers: LCCN 2022048357 (print) | LCCN 2022048358 (ebook) | ISBN 9781590567012 (paperback) | ISBN 9781590567029 (epub)
Subjects: LCSH: Animal rights—Comic books, strips, etc. | BISAC: NATURE / Animal Rights | SOCIAL SCIENCE / Activism & Social Justice | LCGFT: Comics (Graphic works) | Graphic novels.
Classification: LCC PN6727.J345 S25 2023 (print) | LCC PN6727.J345 (ebook) | DDC 741.5/973—dc23/eng/20221017
LC record available at https://lccn.loc.gov/2022048357
LC ebook record available at https://lccn.loc.gov/2022048358

FOR RUSTY

??? — Nov. 10 2020

Foreword

Charles Waltz-Rieber

Veganism presents humans with a frightening but rewarding radicalization of thought and action. It is a crushing disillusionment to pervasive violence. It is also the awakening of a rich and deep tenderness. My journey with veganism has been one of my most challenging and humbling experiences, bringing me perspective that lives as both ongoing trauma and its unending work towards reconciliation. Connecting with non-humans, learning from them and seeing their personhood as it exists across all species, has taught me a full, enriching love. It is knowing this love that has shown me loss, loss that invariably expands as long as my capacity to mourn it does. Veganism is bringing my actions to congruence with these feelings and values, it is learning the realities of immense violence so that I can learn to love its non-human victims more honestly and impactfully.

SALT is about the fervent distress of grief and hope uniting to motivate animal activism. Reading it, I felt the exhaustion of grieving banal violence as well as the meditativeness of caring for someone liberated from it. Written with a candor that is simultaneously humorous in its neurosis and devastating in its well justified fear, there is an immediacy to the characters' troubling relationships to activism. Coyote captures the vulnerability of forming relationships around shared activist values, how conflict between people with shared goals but different means has greater consequences when those goals pertain to someone else's life. With *SALT*, Coyote confesses a moment of burn out in the face of uncertainty, cynicism, and seemingly unresolvable trauma. But ultimately, *SALT* is an expression of the love and tenderness veganism is founded on because it is a story of dedication and endurance. There may never be one clear answer on how to sustainably commit ourselves to non-humans, there is only perseverance and feeding our love. This story is not about how to make the right choices on behalf of non-humans, but about the weight of caring for life that should have never been ours to manipulate. I've read it more times than I can count, and it has yet to lose its catharsis.

Charles Waltz-Rieber is an illustrator and printmaker based in Brooklyn, printing at lucky risograph. His publication experience allows him to explore a variety of both visual and text based prints, zines, and artist books.

CHAPTER 1

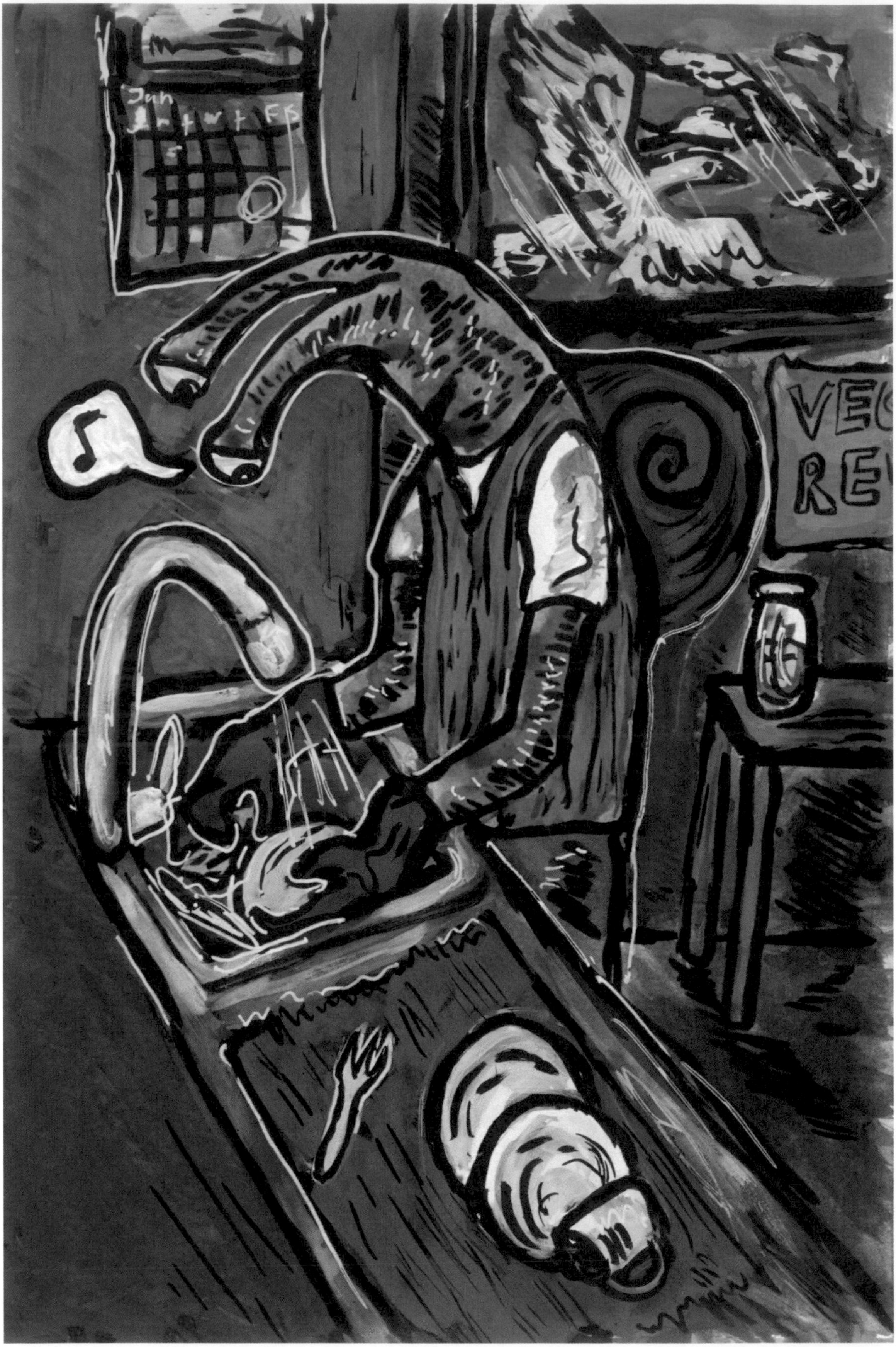
Jan

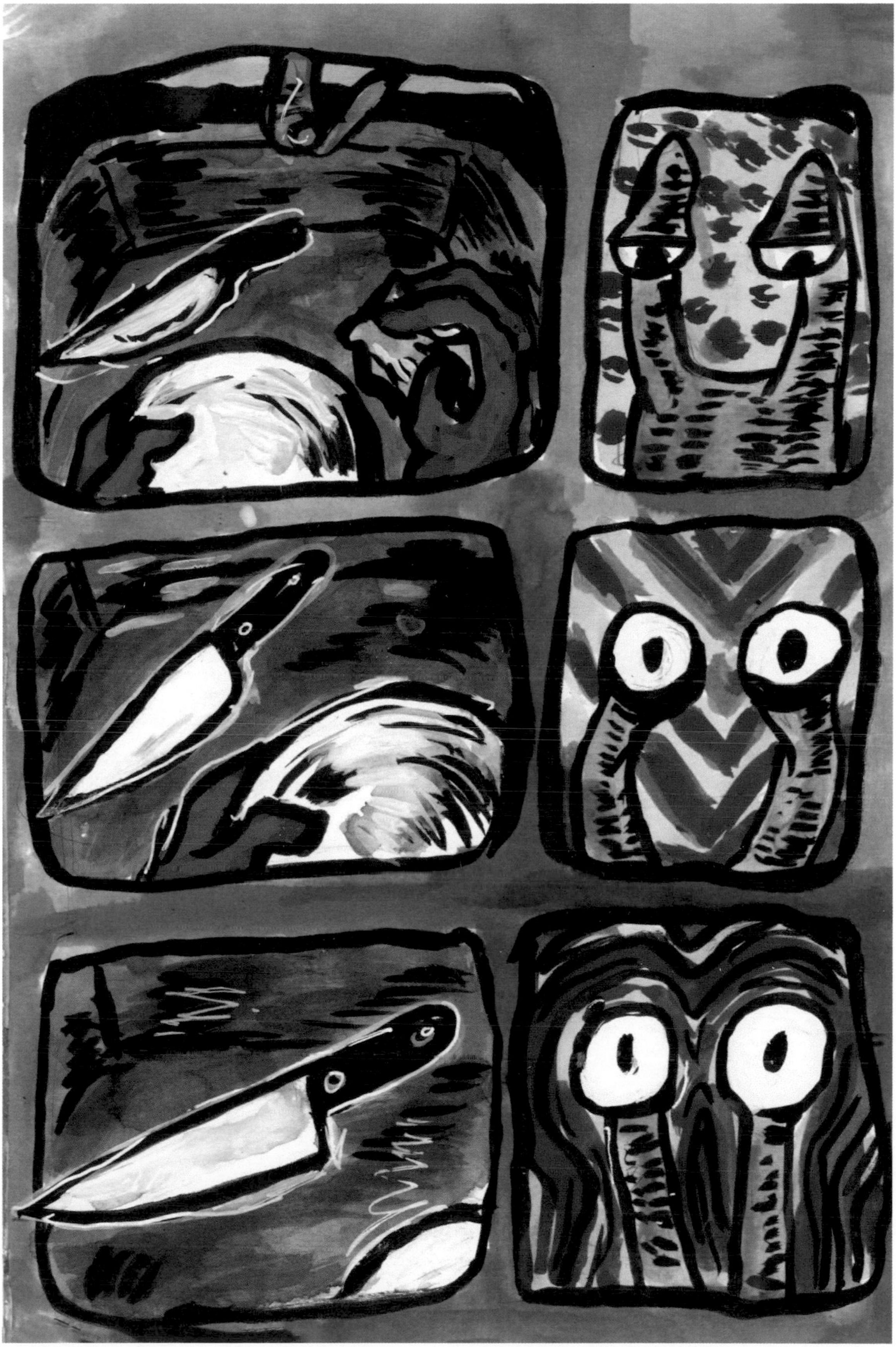

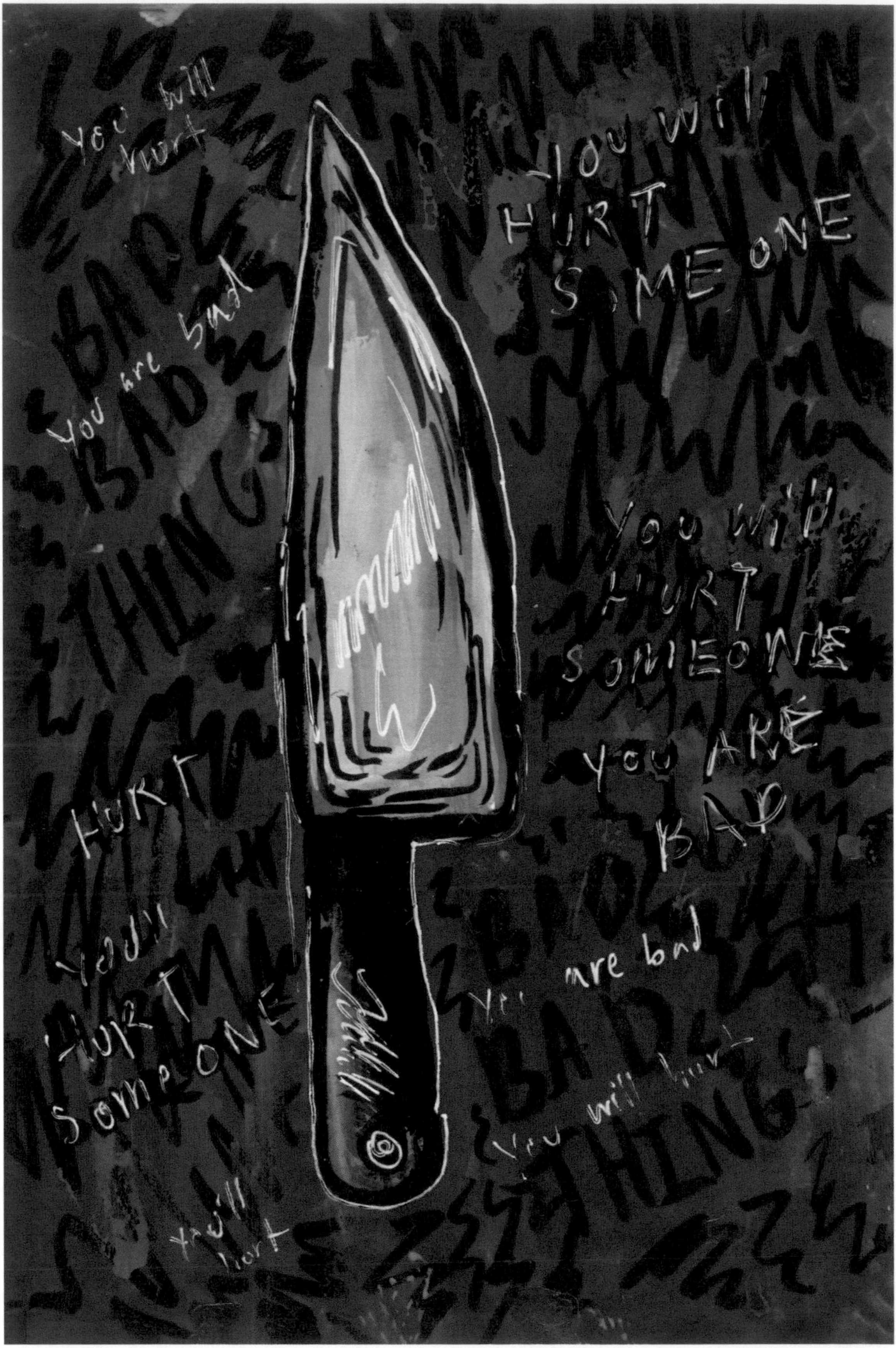
You will hurt
You will HURT SOMEONE
You are bad
BAD THING
You will HURT SOMEONE
YOU ARE BAD
HURT
You HURT SOMEONE
You are bad
BAD THING!
You will hurt
You'll hurt

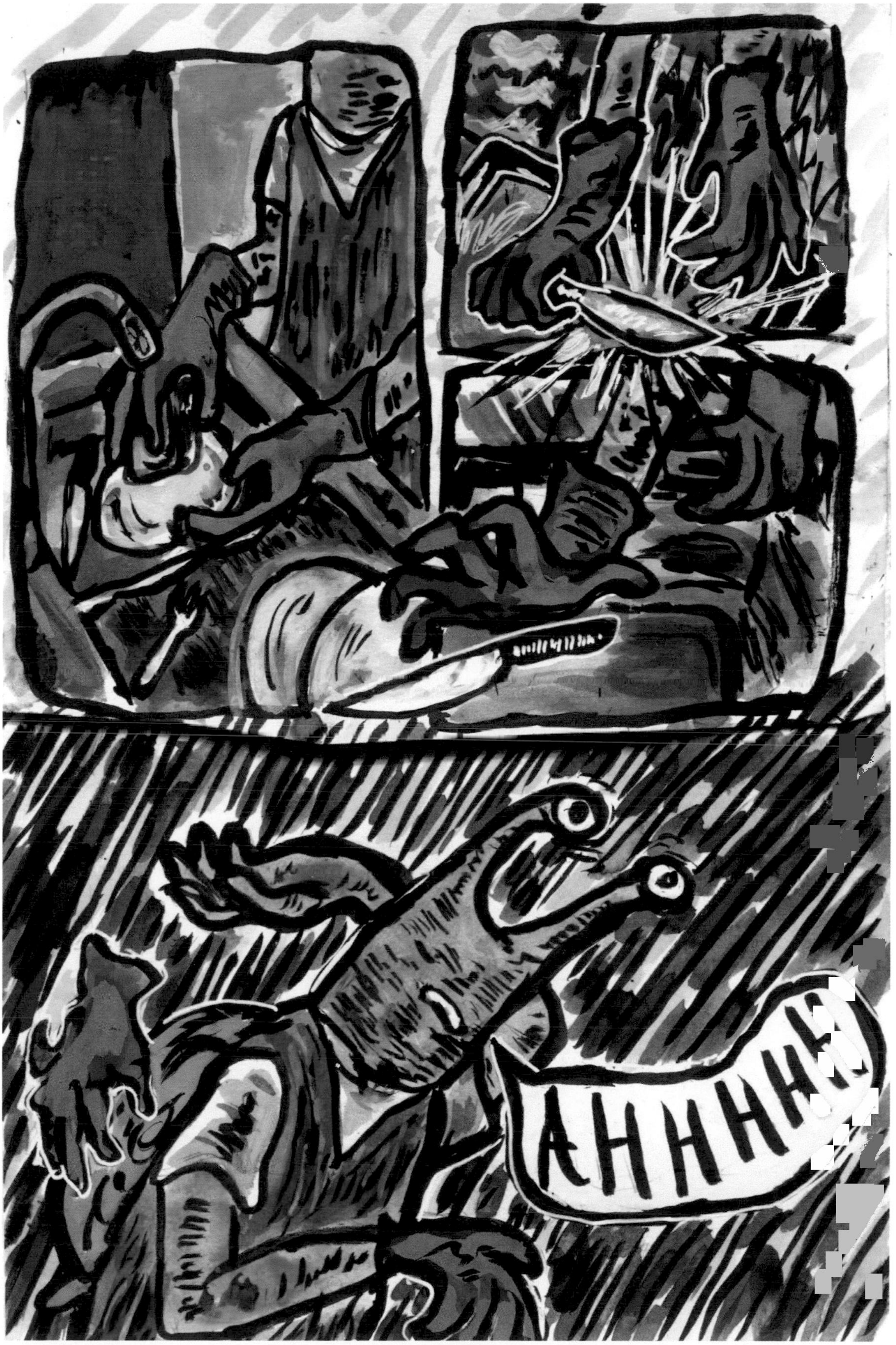
AHHHHH

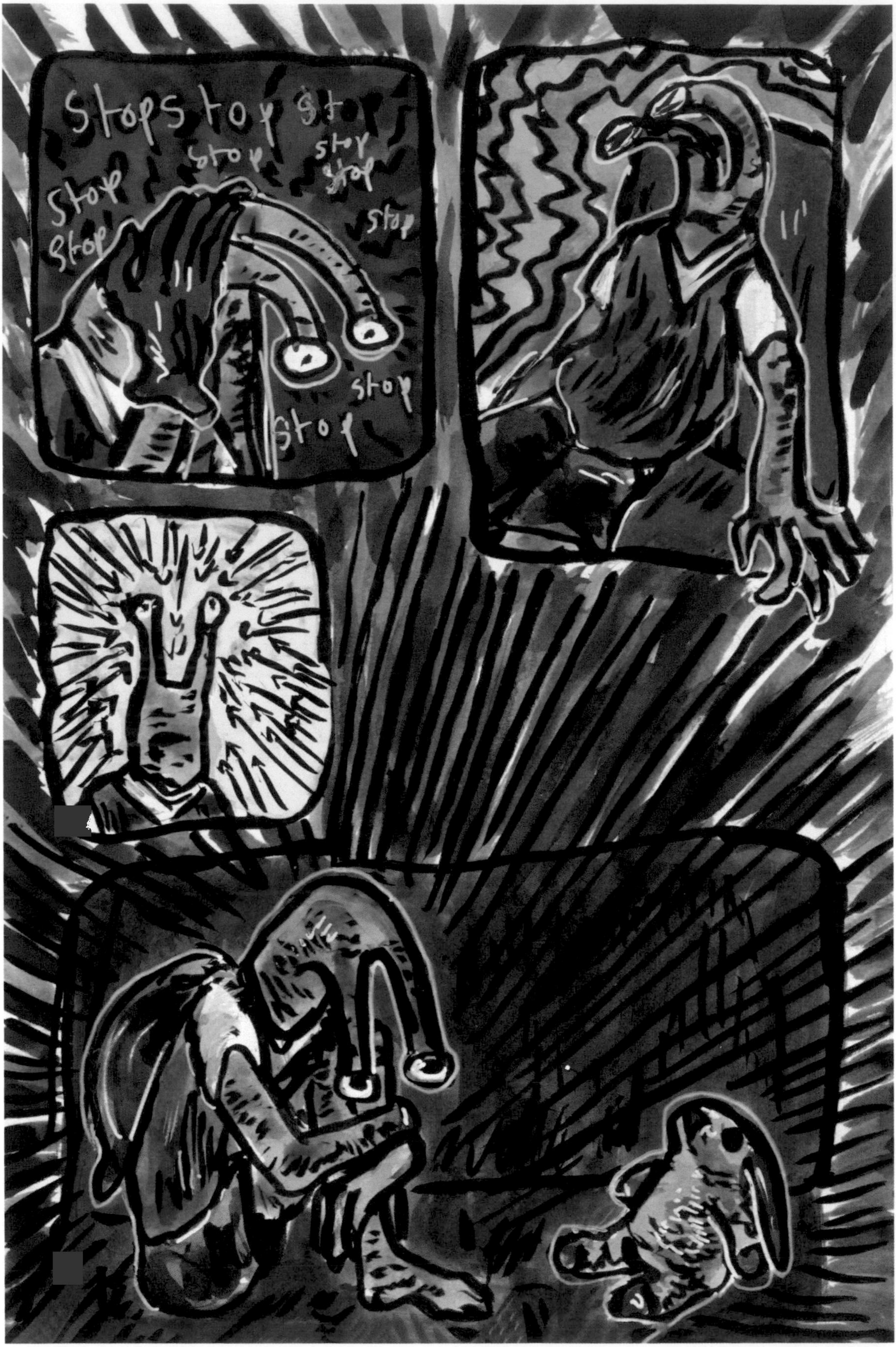
Stopstop sto
stop
stop
stop
stop
stop
stop
stop
stop
stop

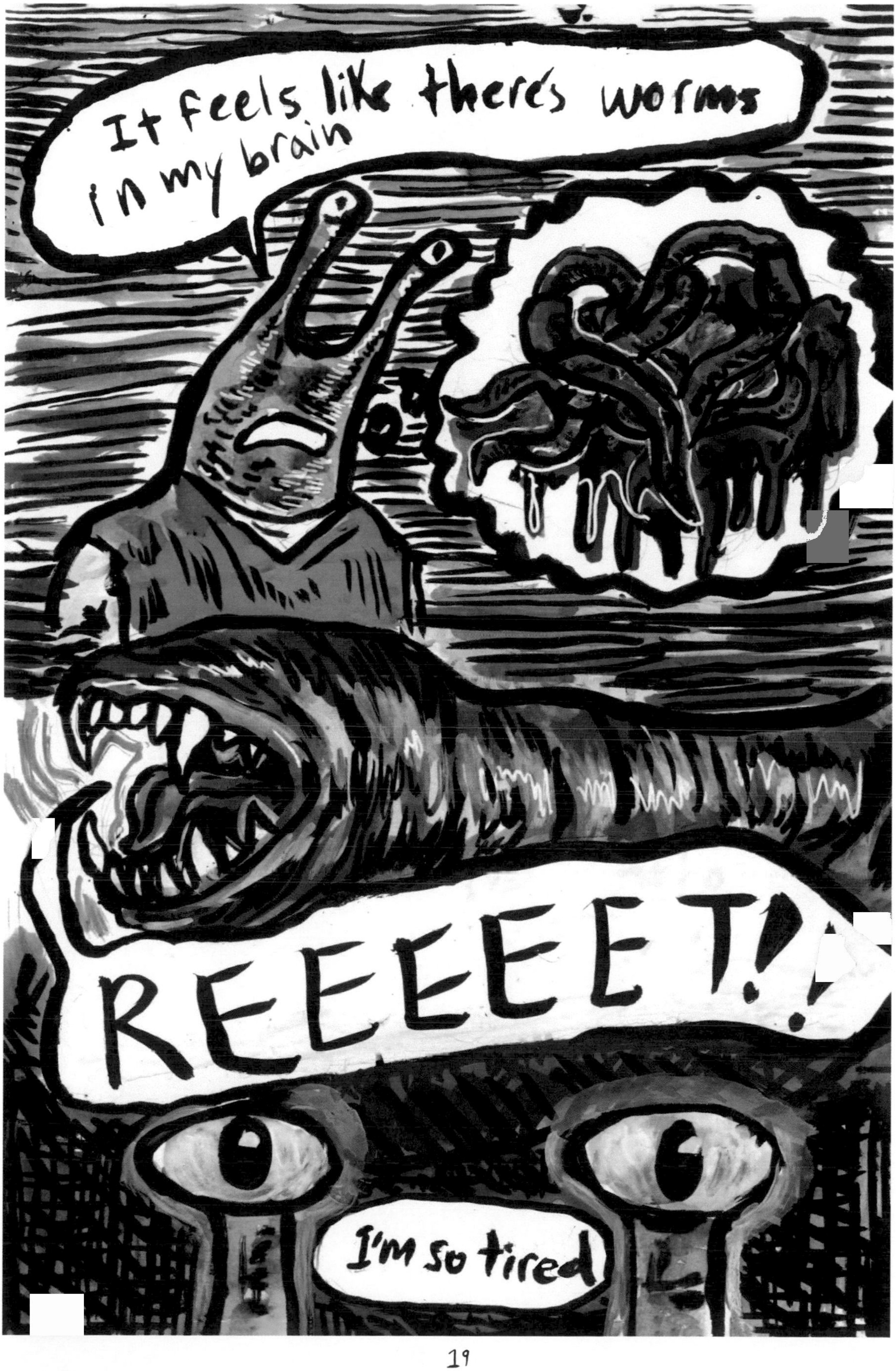
It feels like there's worms in my brain
REEEEET!!
I'm so tired

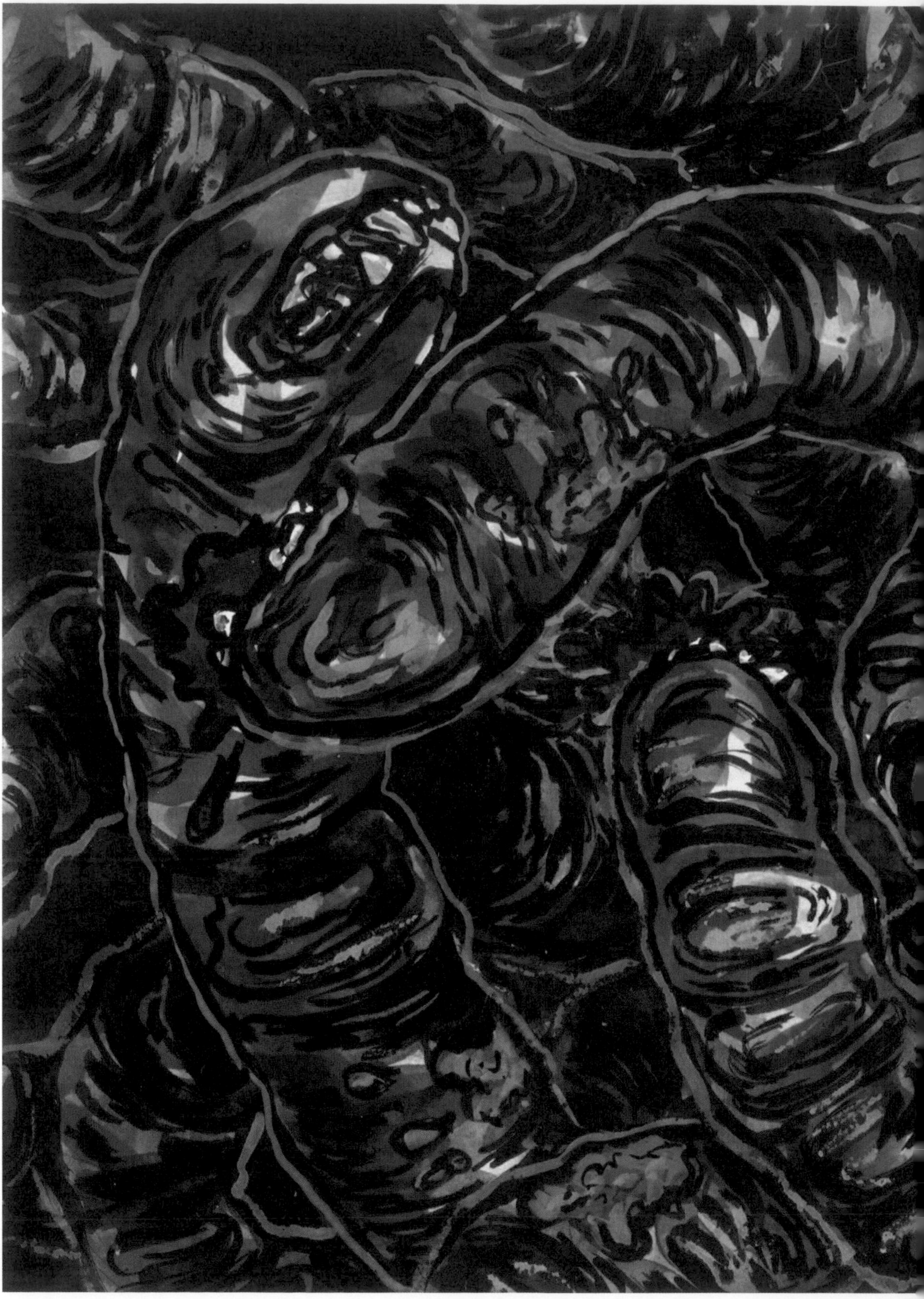

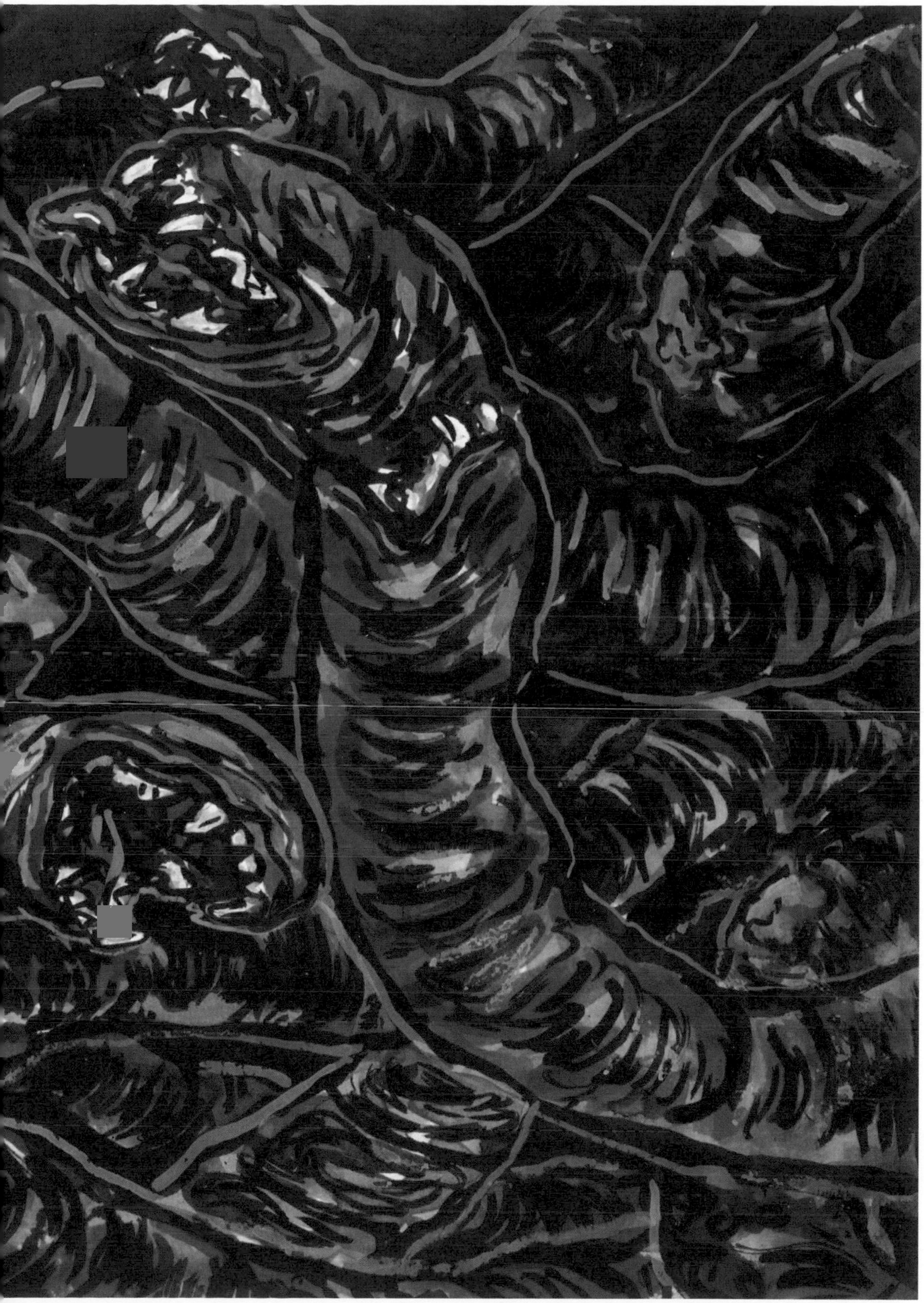

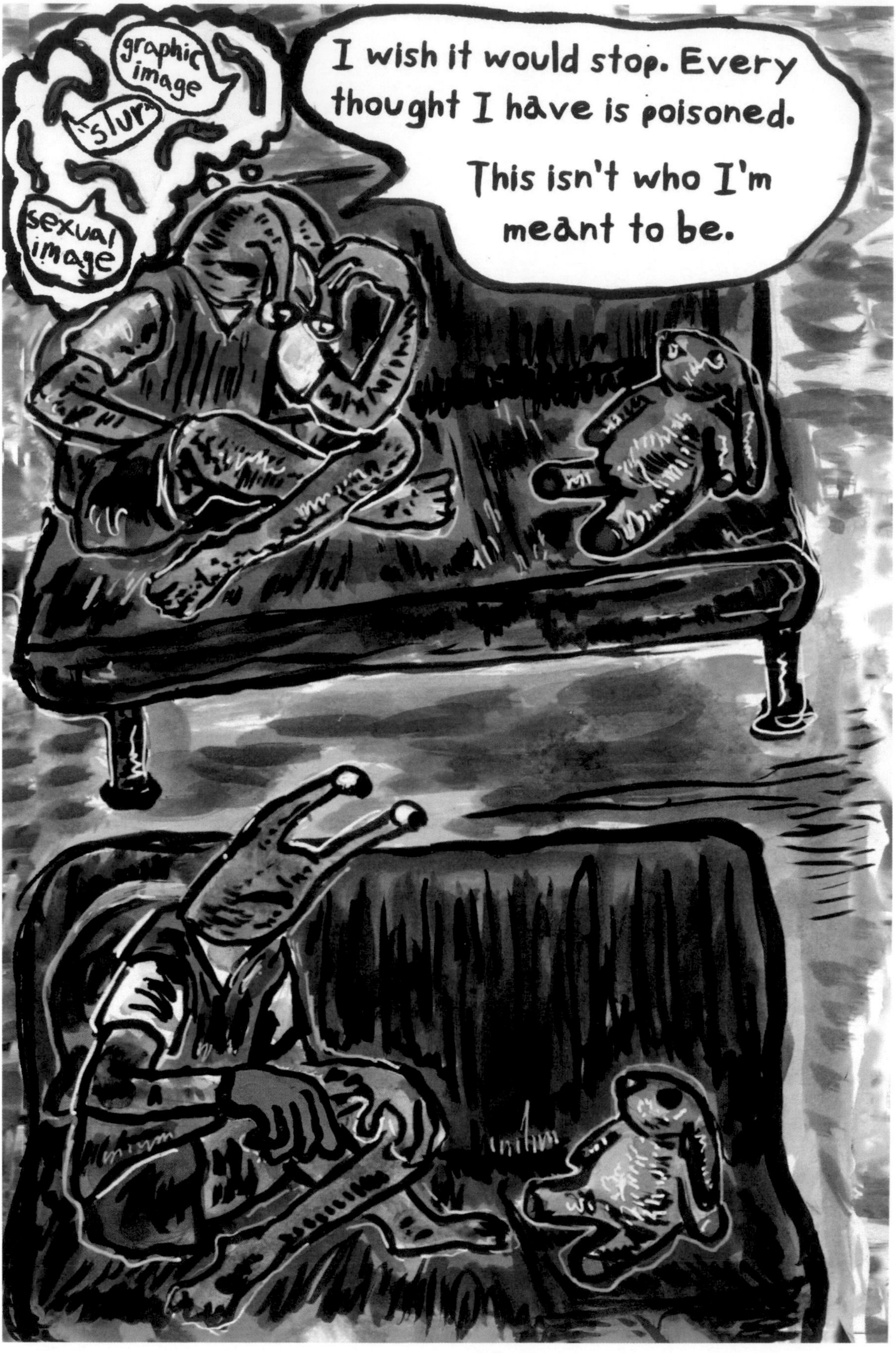
graphic image
slur
sexual image
I wish it would stop. Every thought I have is poisoned.
This isn't who I'm meant to be.

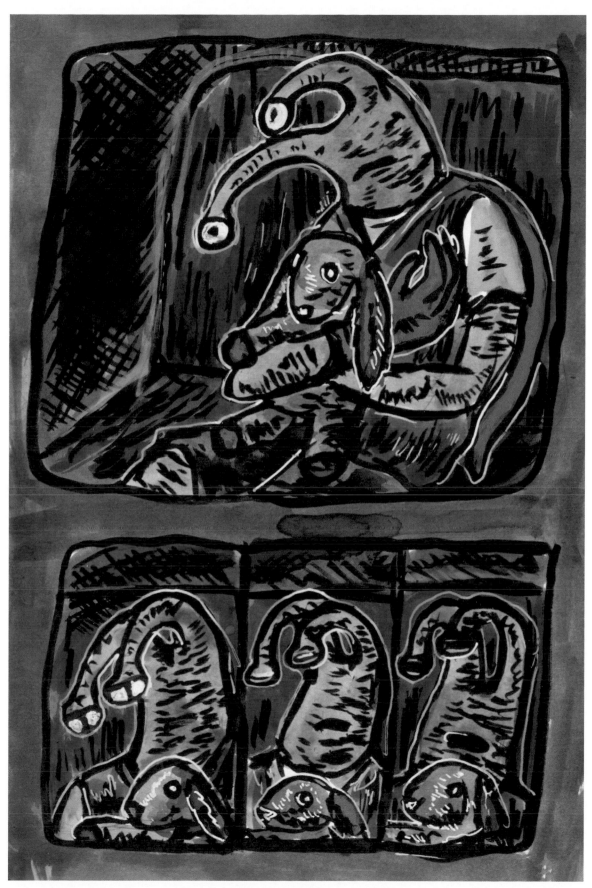

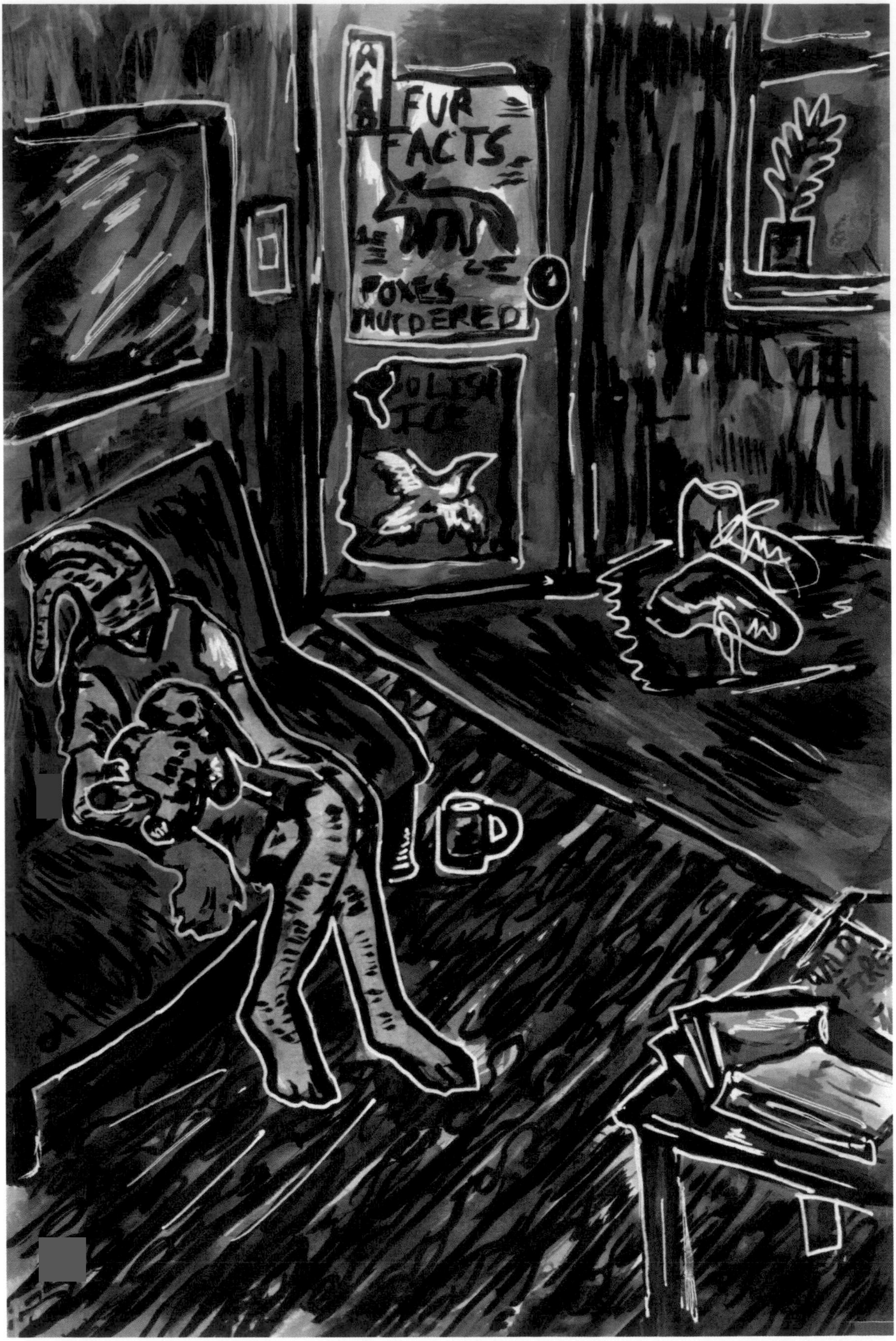
FUR FACTS
FOXES MURDERED!

CHAPTER 2

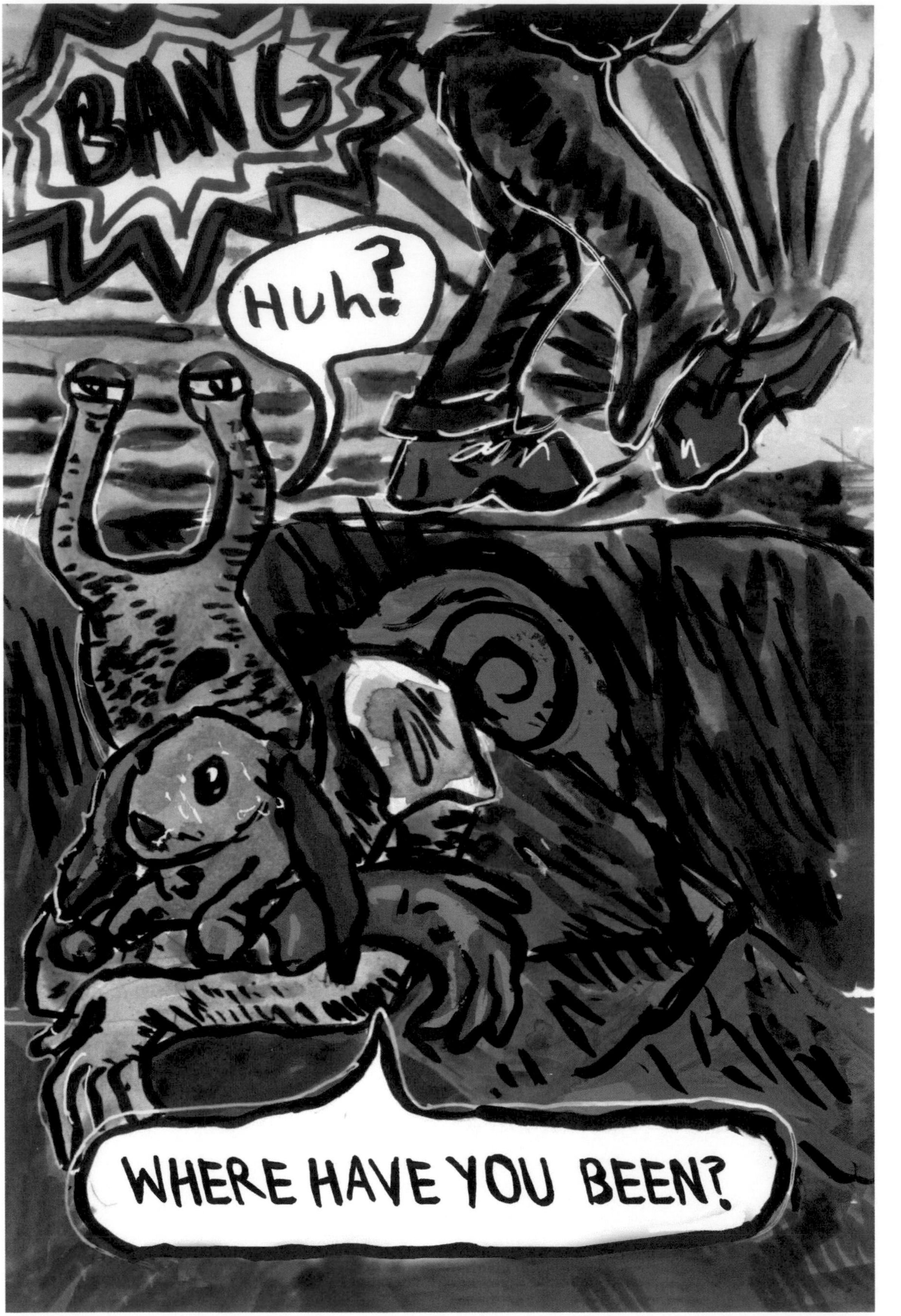
BANG
Huh?
WHERE HAVE YOU BEEN?

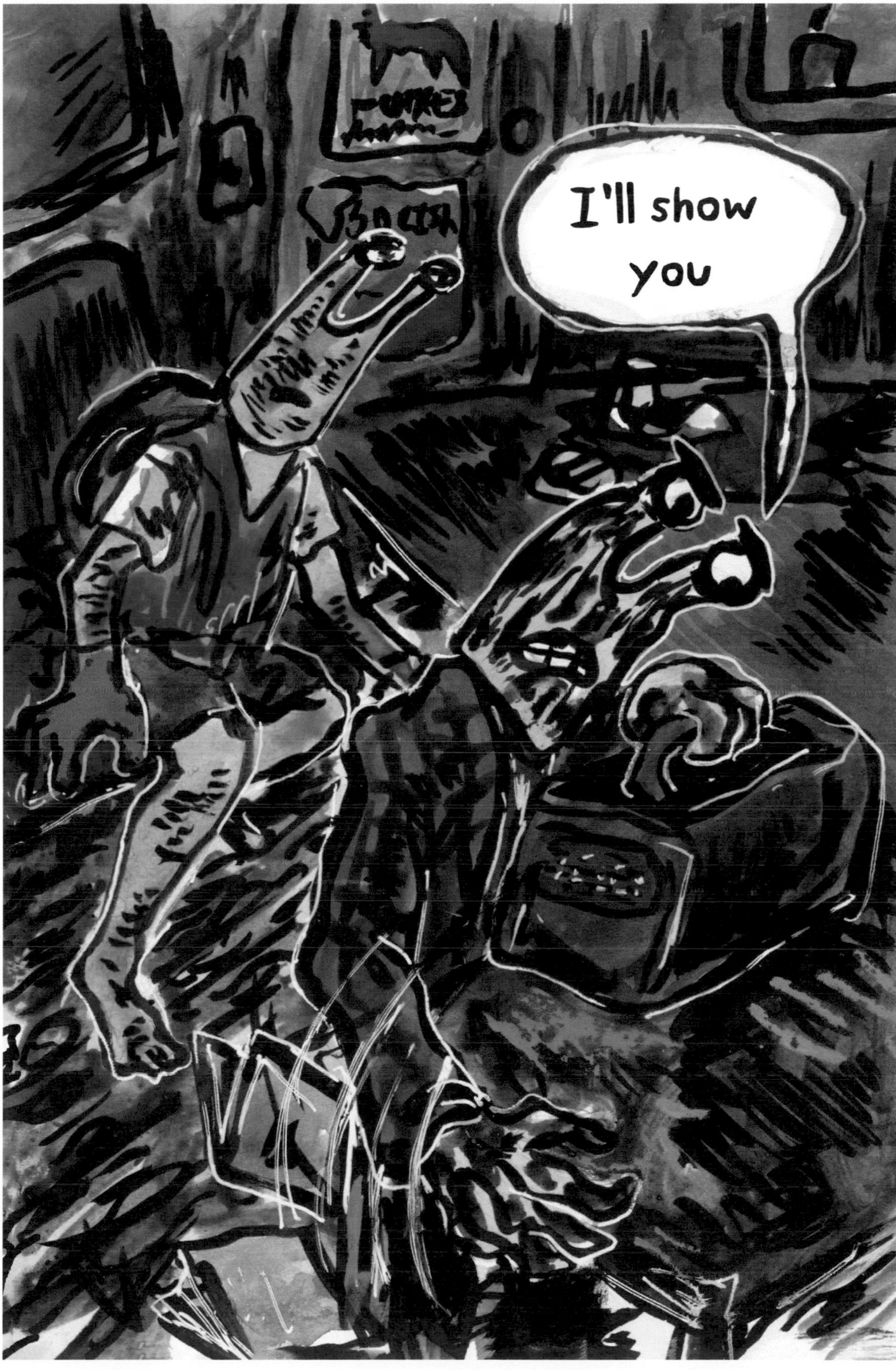
I'll show you

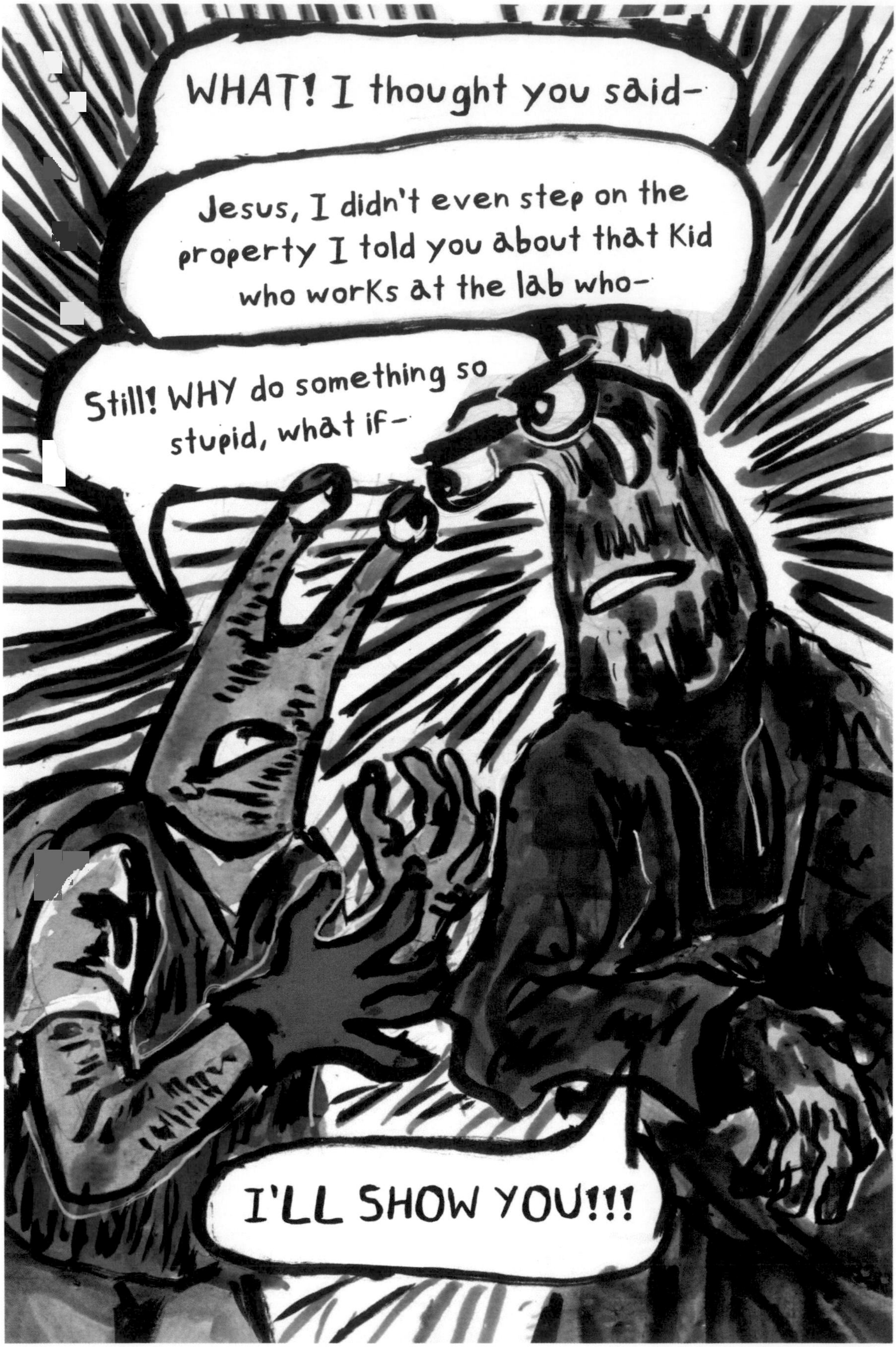
WHAT! I thought you said-
Jesus, I didn't even step on the property I told you about that Kid who works at the lab who-
Still! WHY do something so stupid, what if-
I'LL SHOW YOU!!!

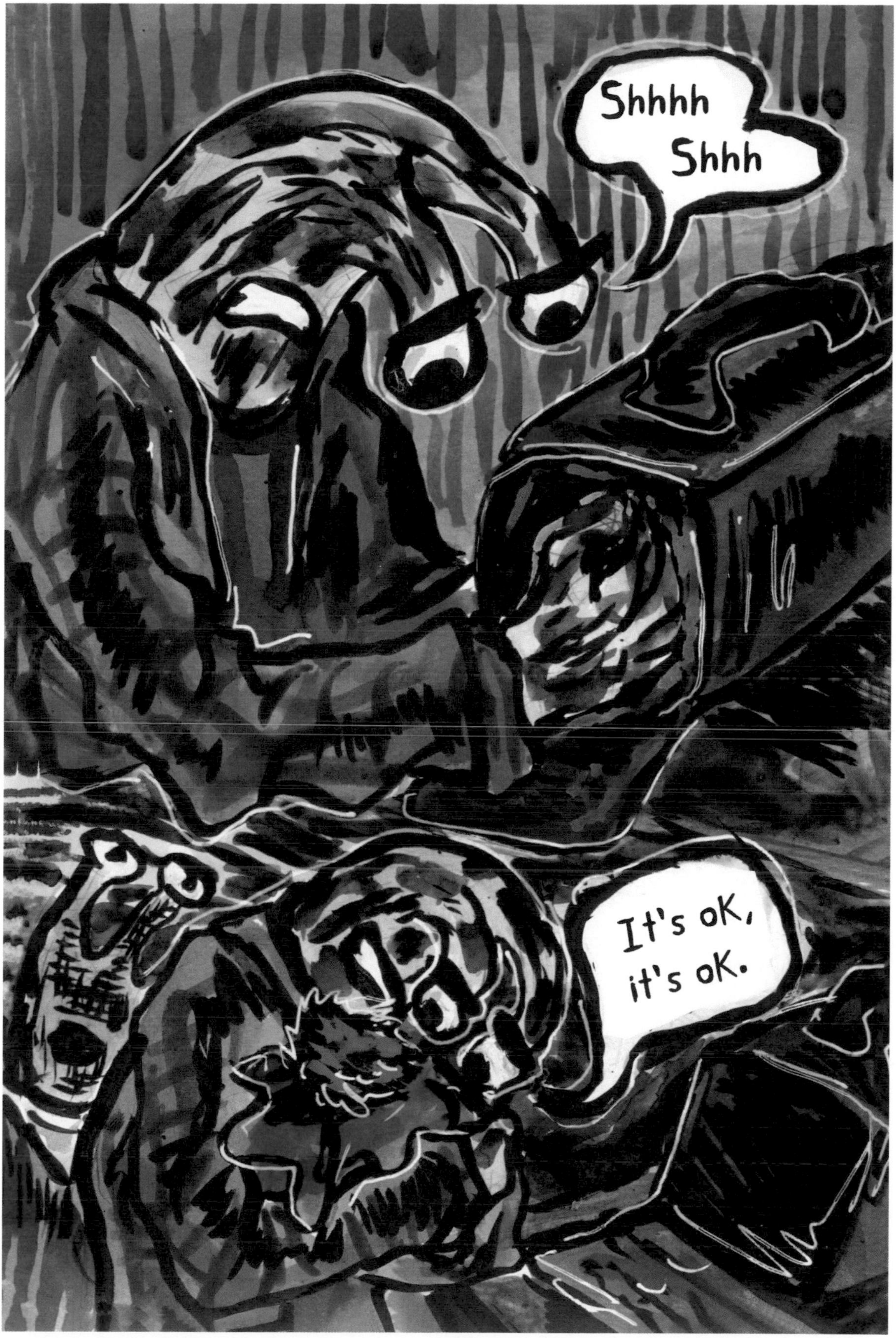
Shhhh Shhh
It's oK, it's oK.

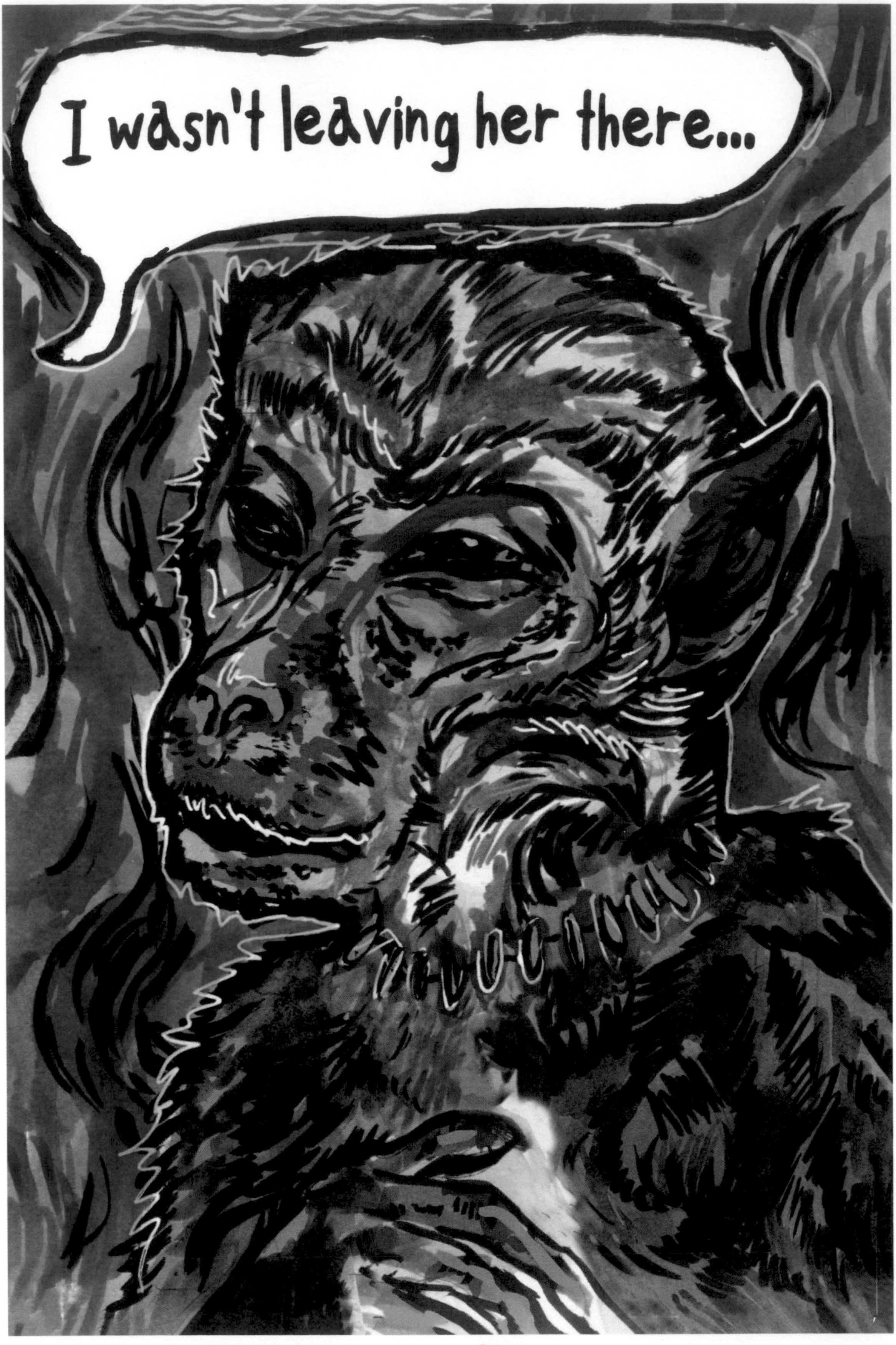
I wasn't leaving her there...

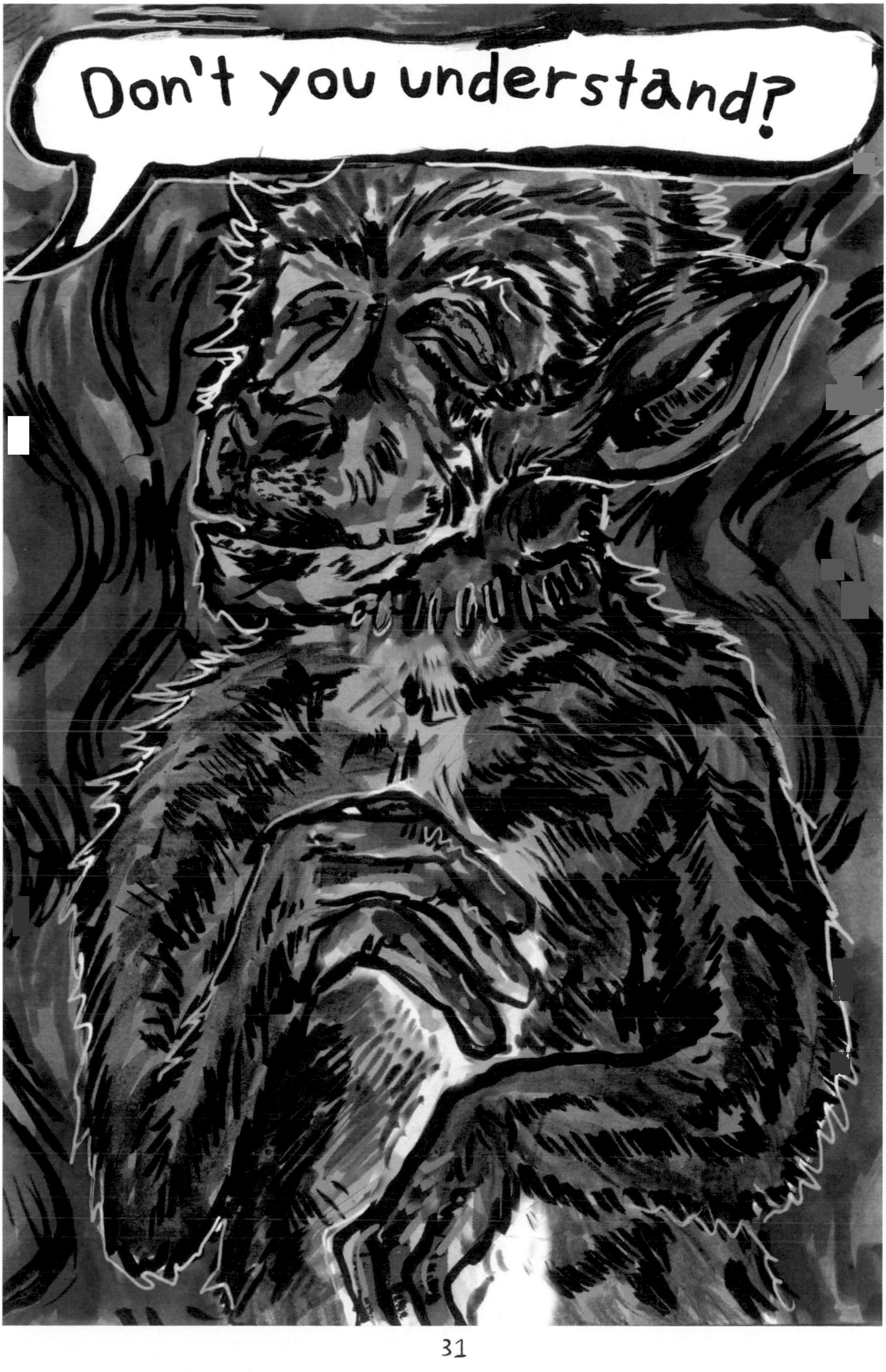
Don't you understand?

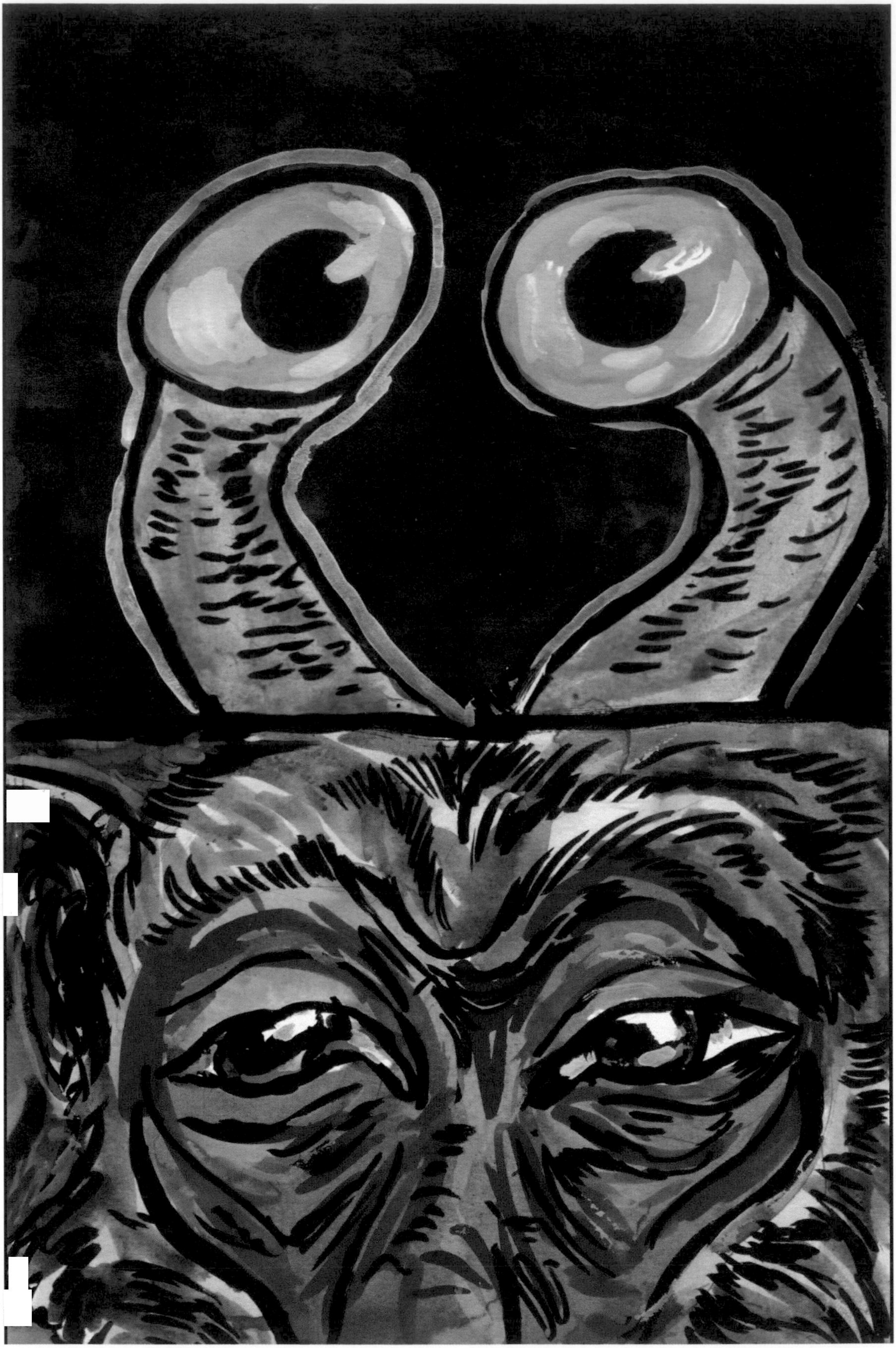

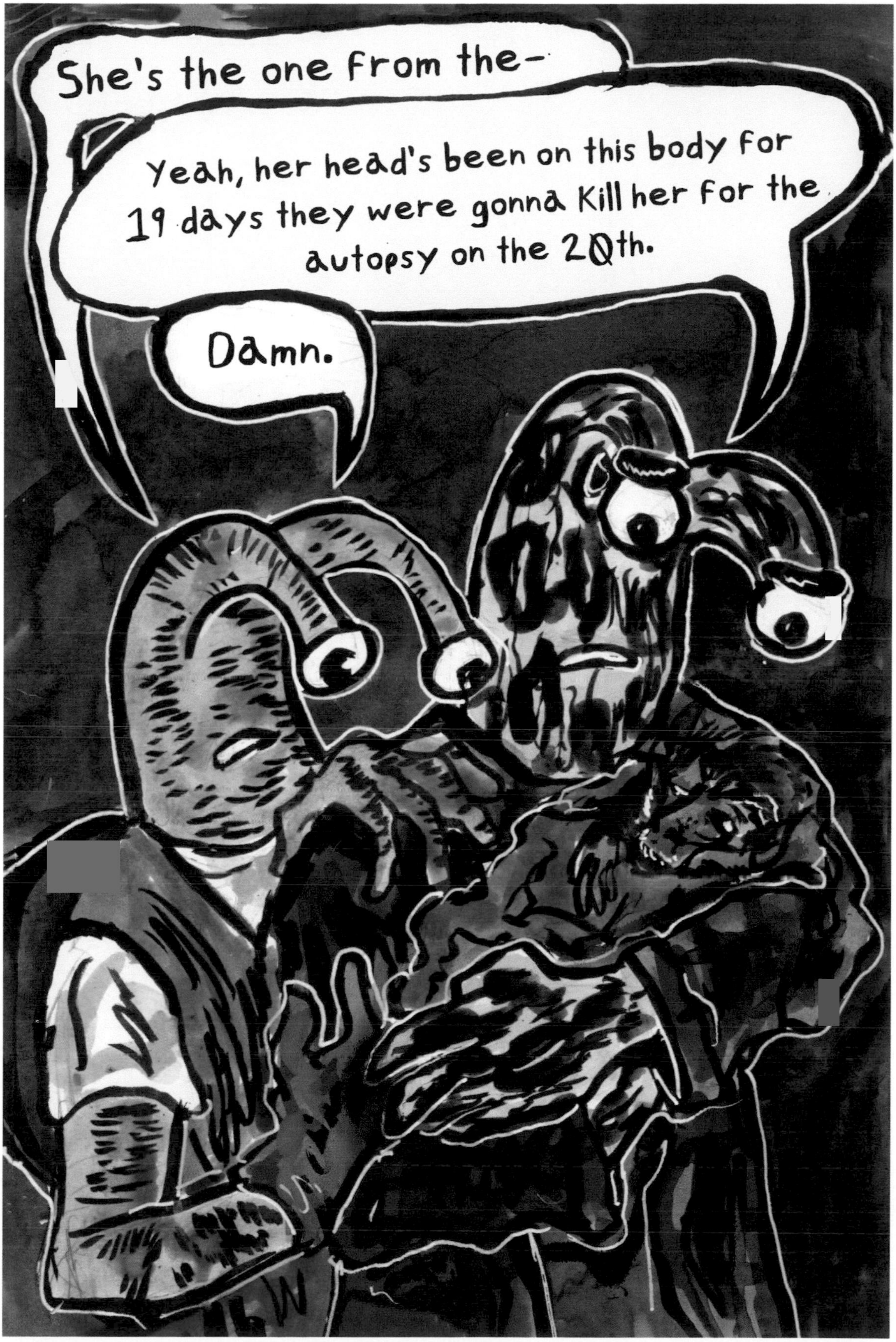
She's the one from the-
Yeah, her head's been on this body for 19 days they were gonna Kill her for the autopsy on the 20th.
Damn.

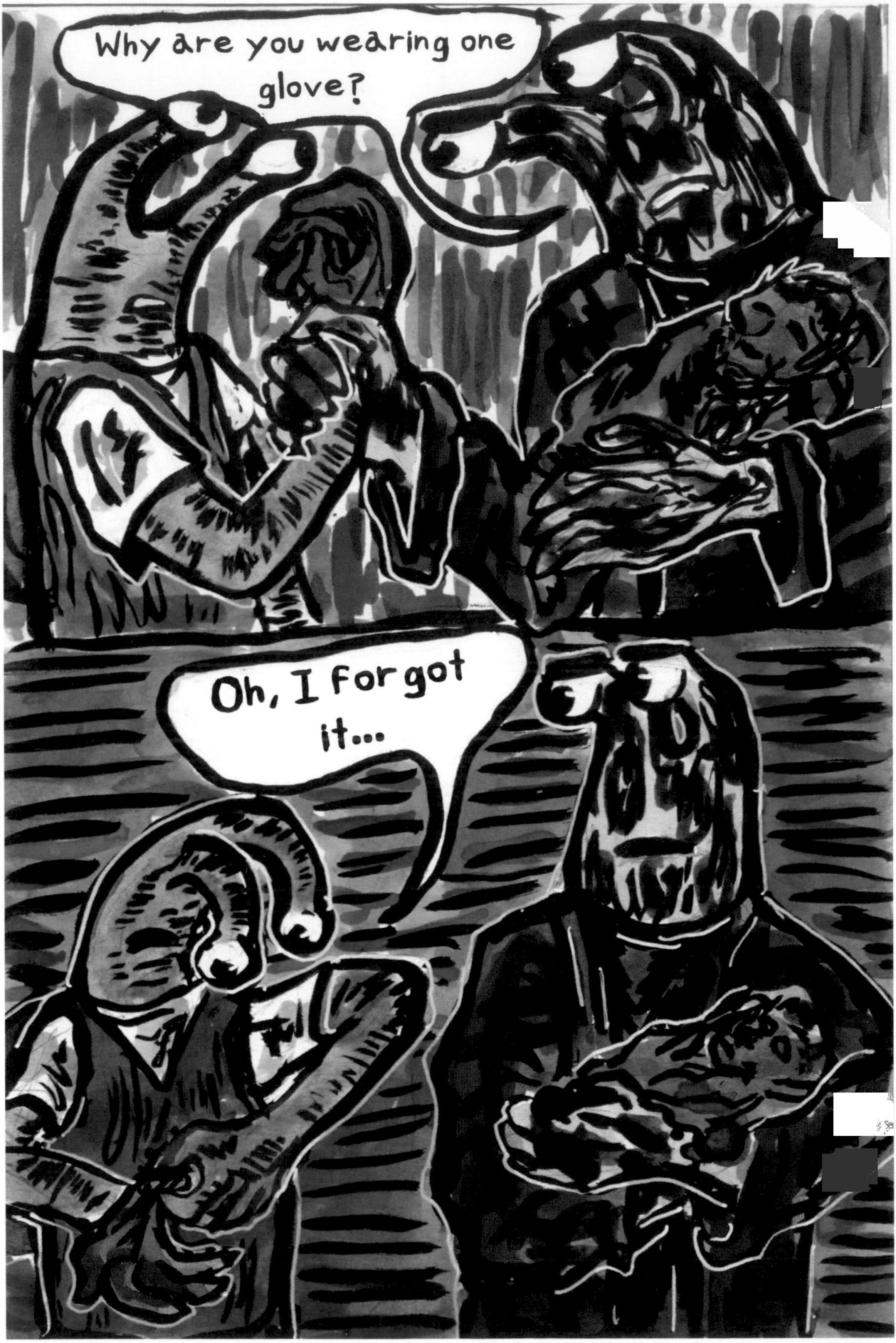
Why are you wearing one glove?
Oh, I forgot it...

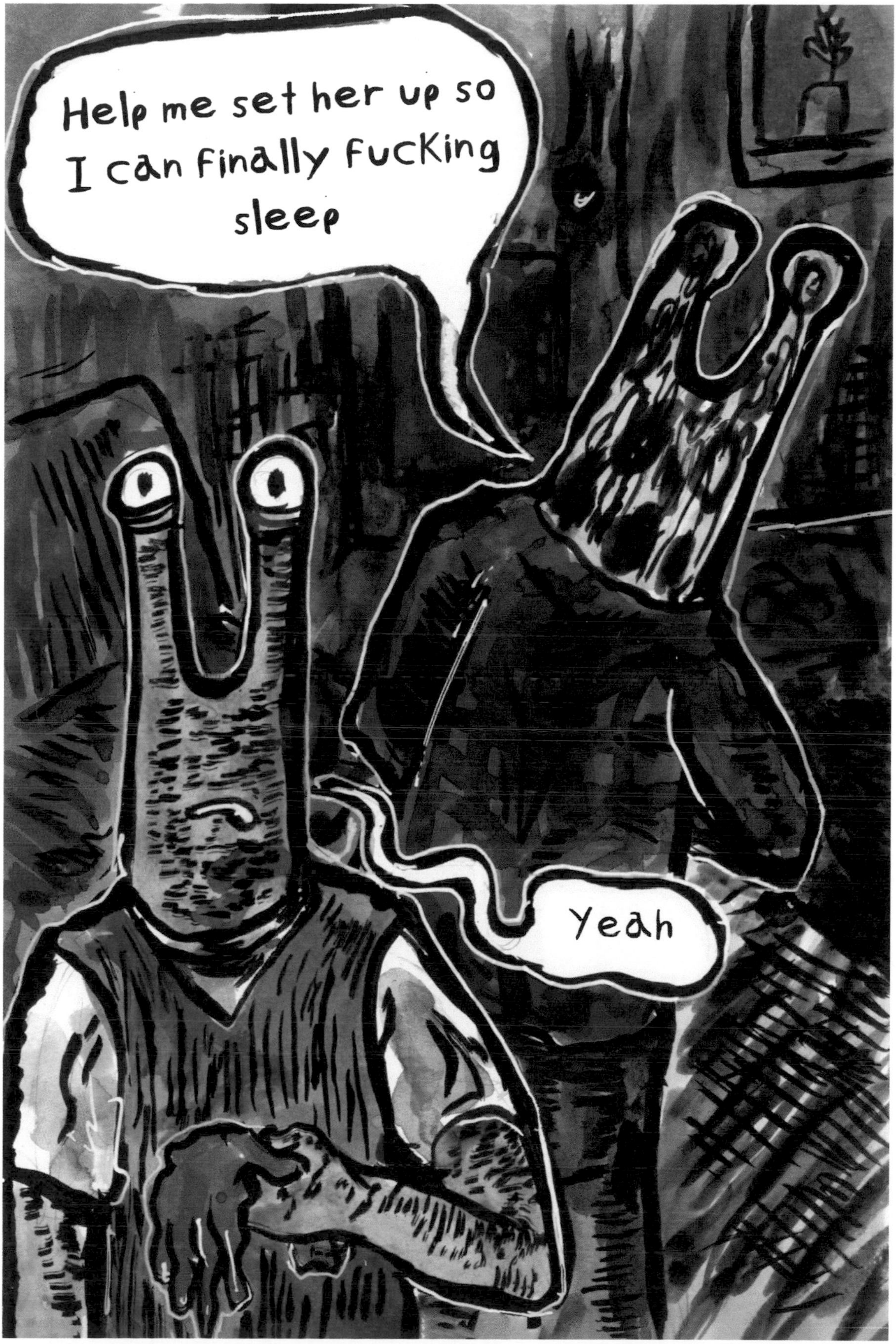
Help me set her up so I can finally fucking sleep
Yeah

CHAPTER
3

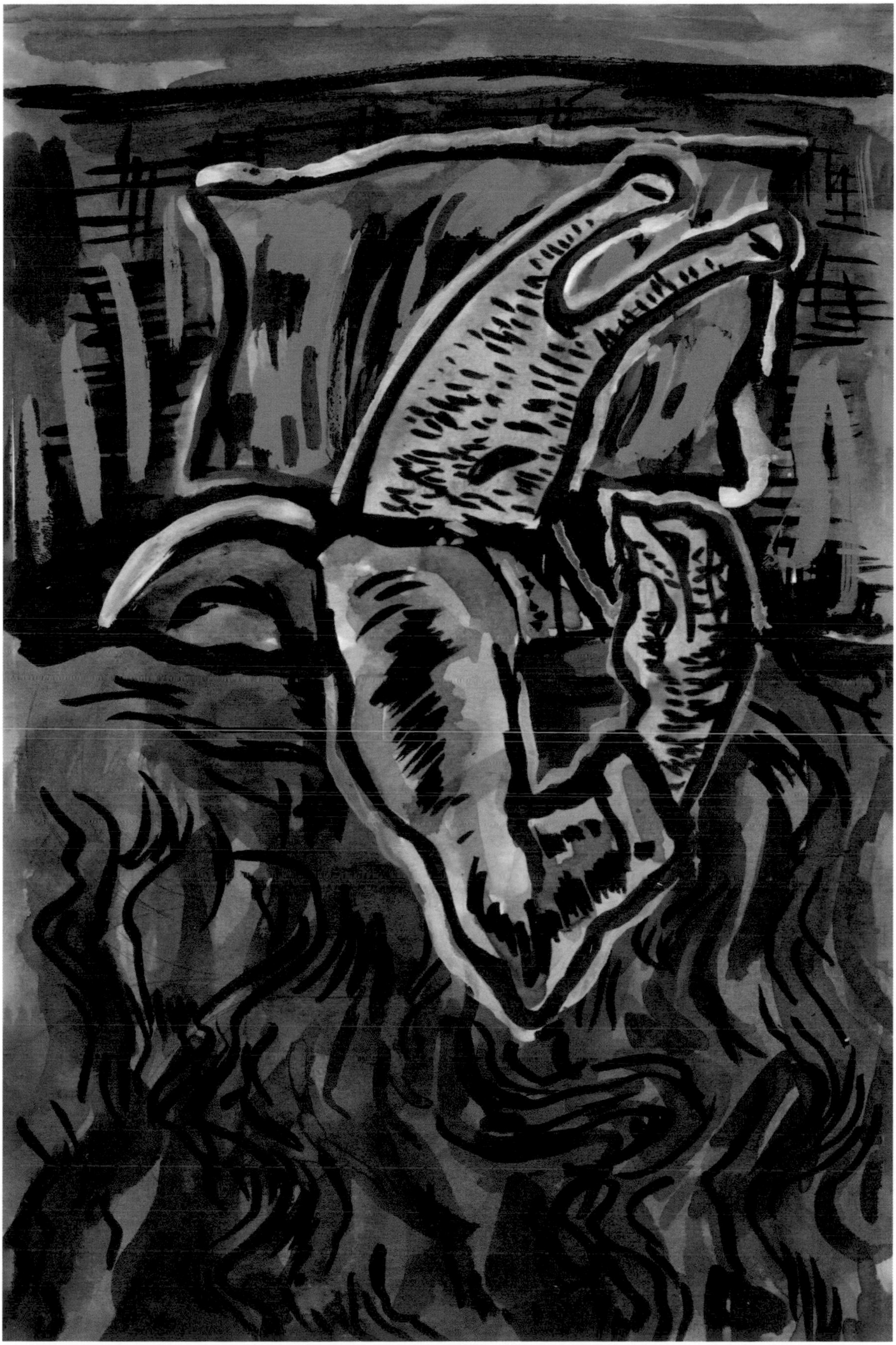

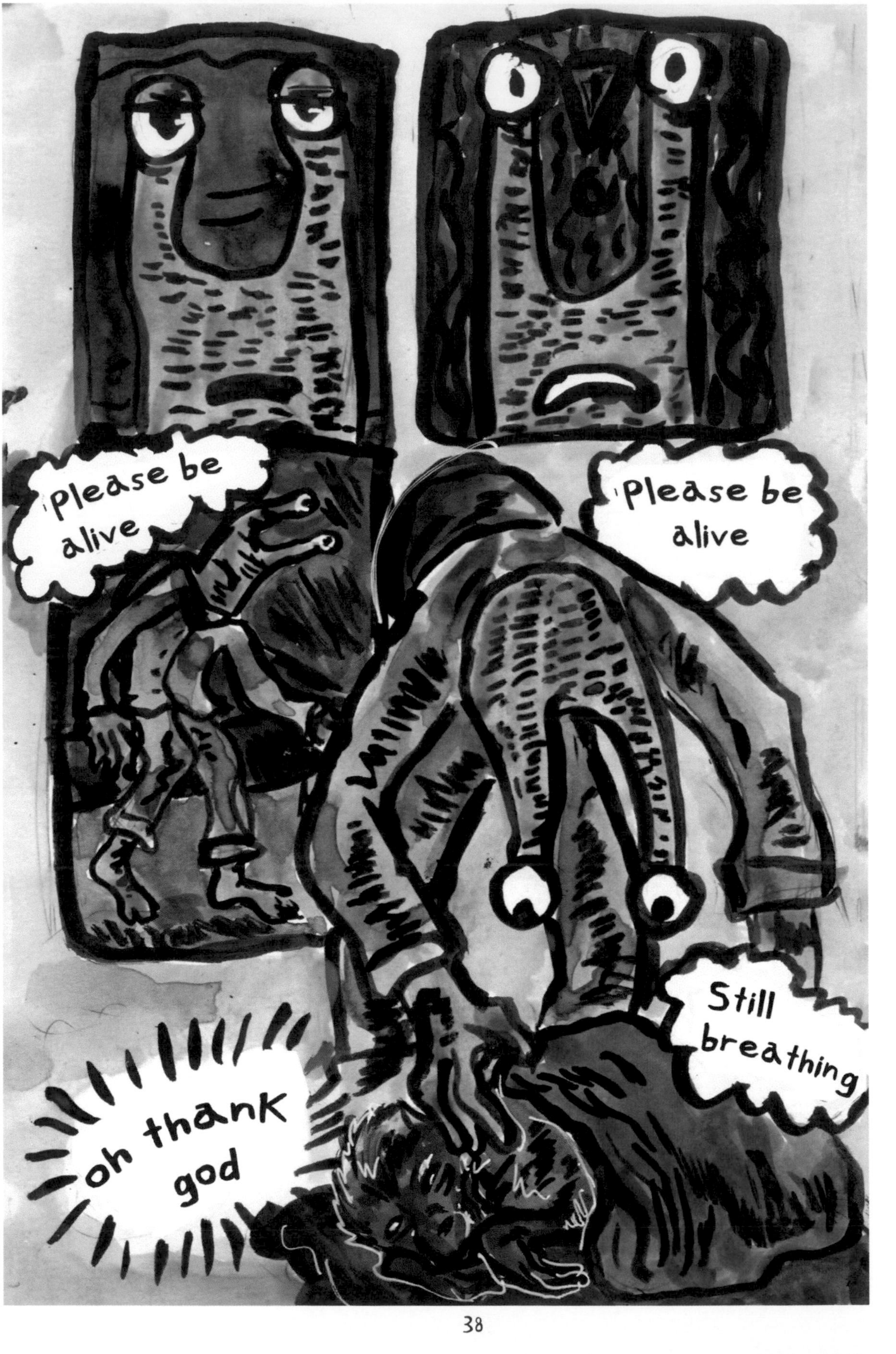
Please be alive
Please be alive
Still breathing
oh thank god

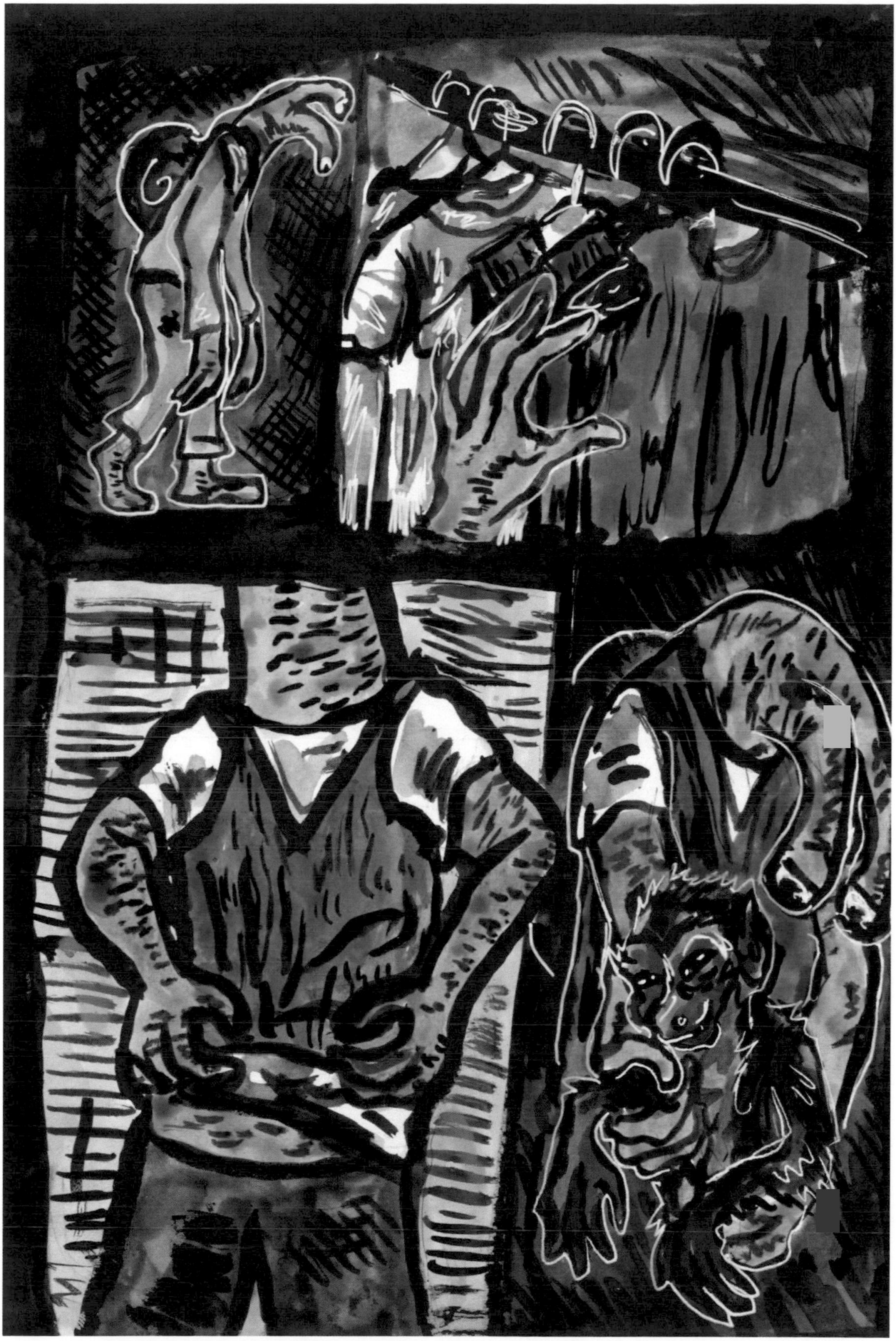

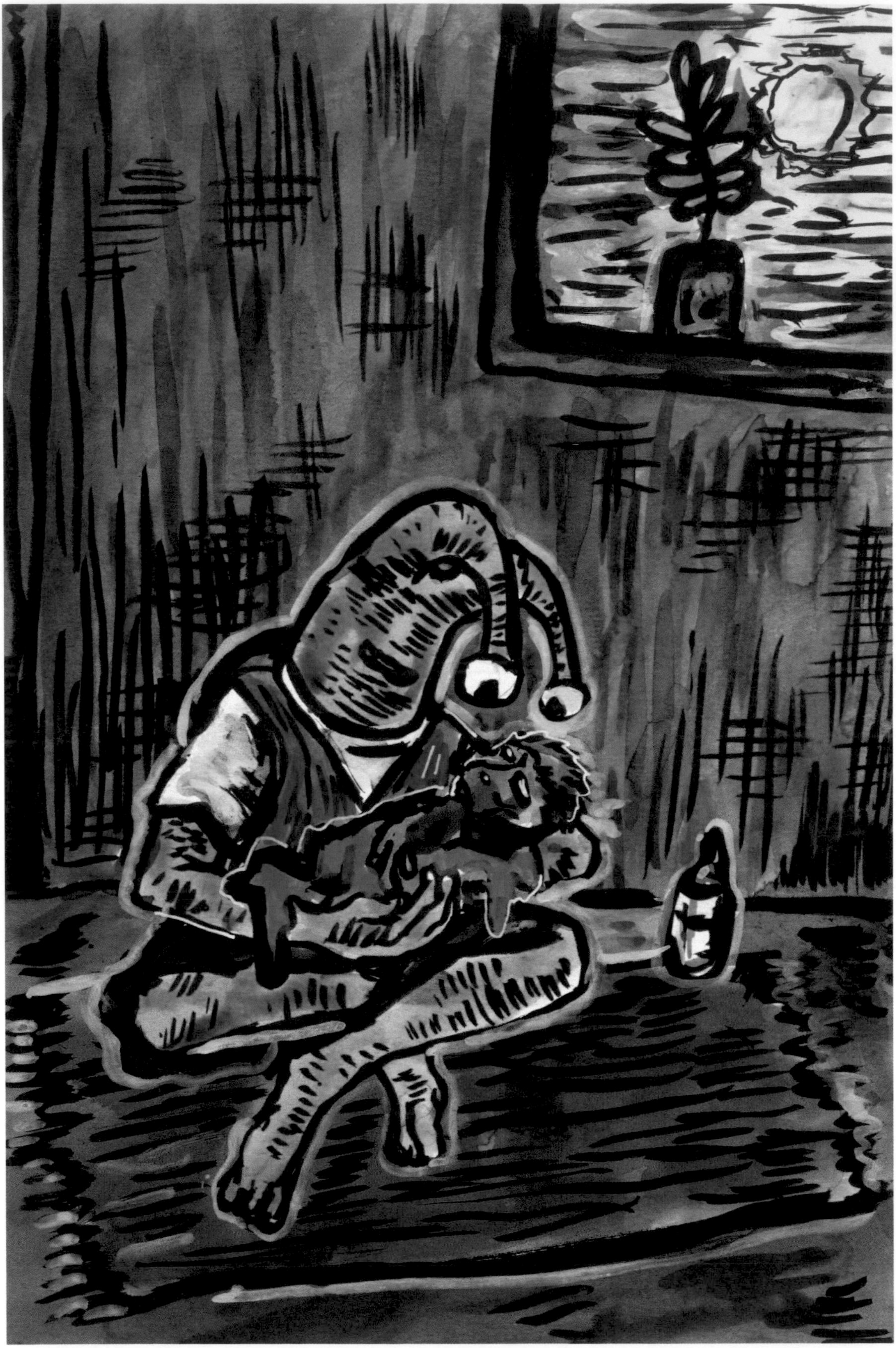

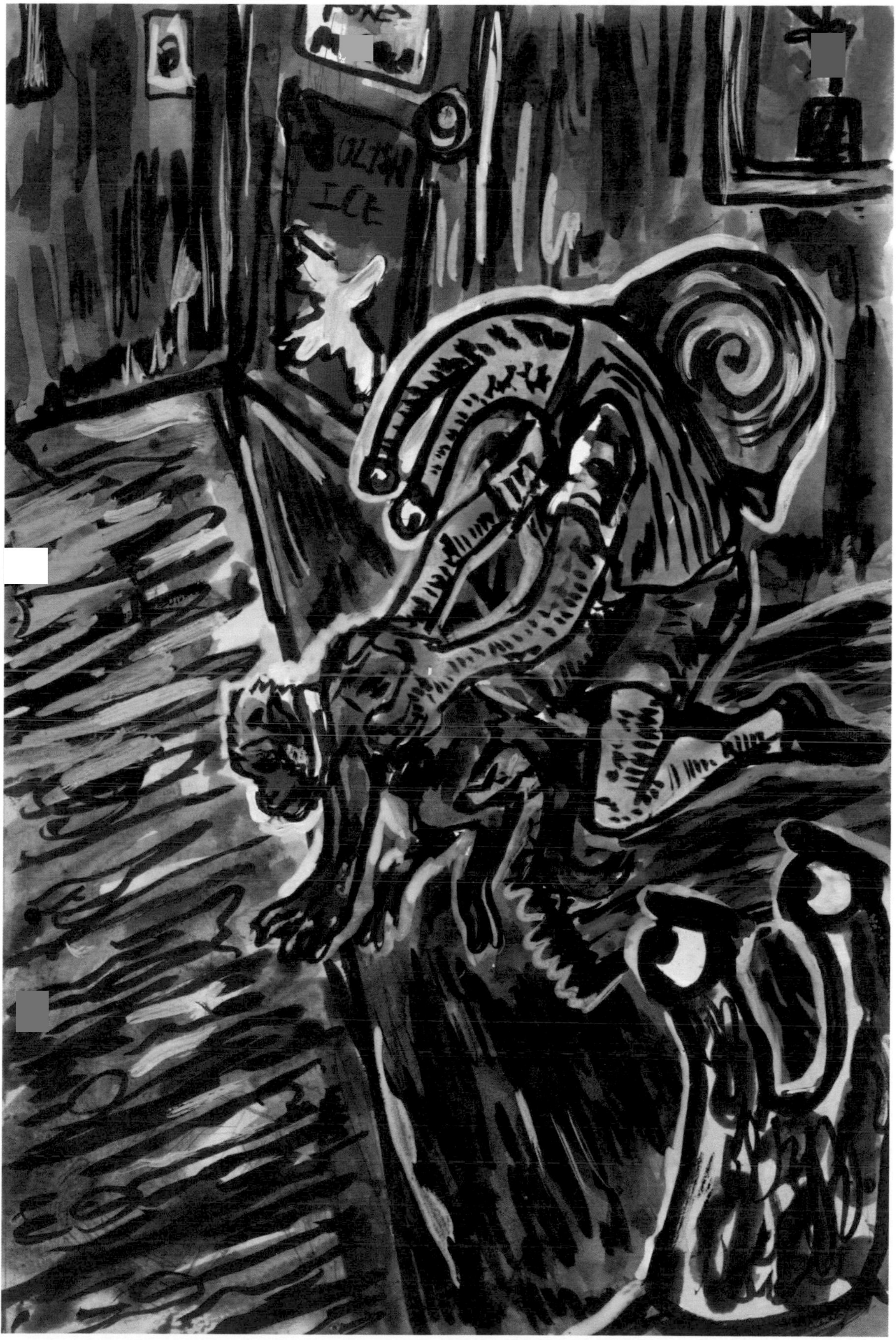
OLISH
ICE

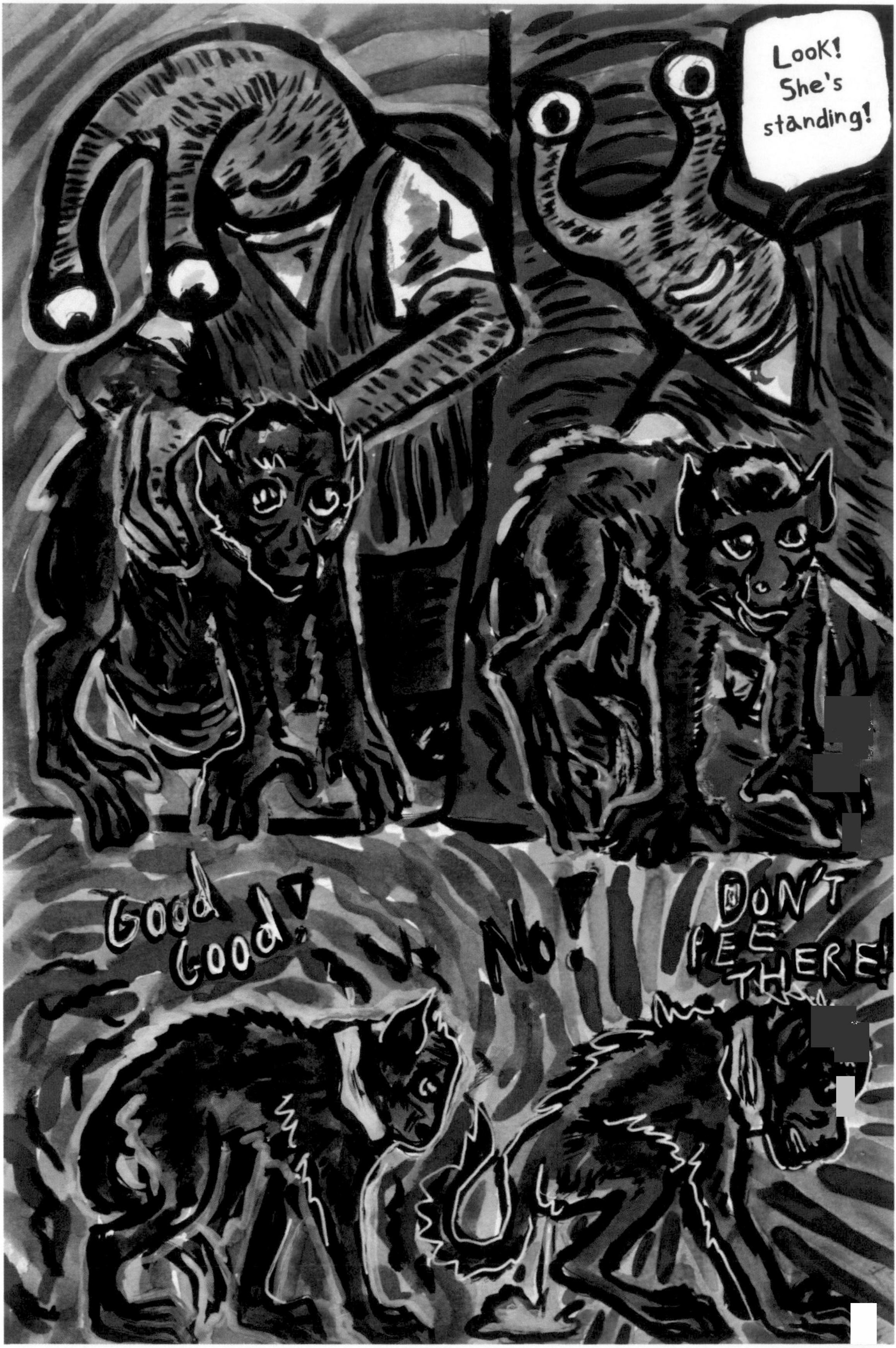
Look! She's standing!
Good Good!
No!
DON'T PEE THERE!

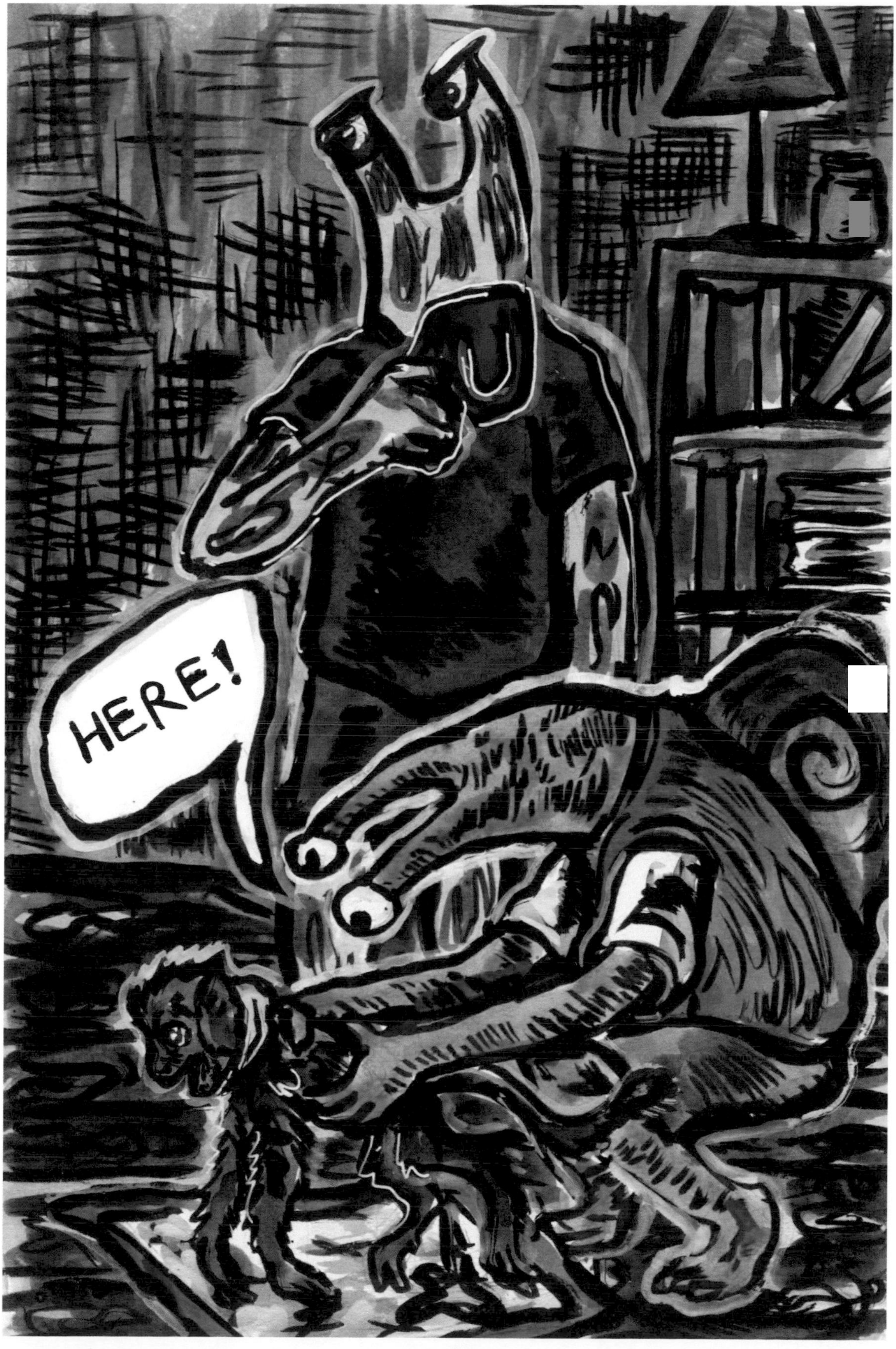
HERE!

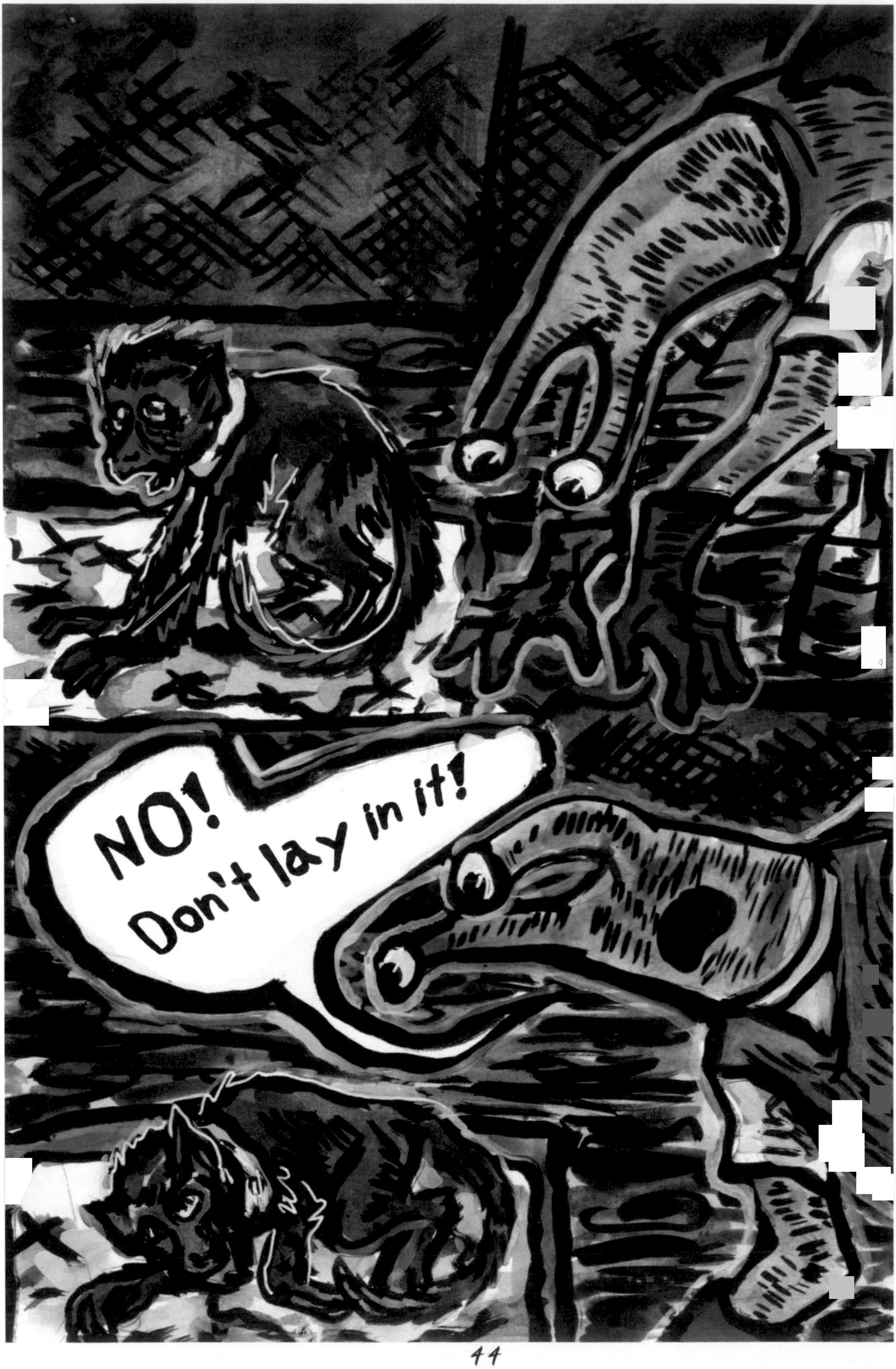
NO! Don't lay in it!

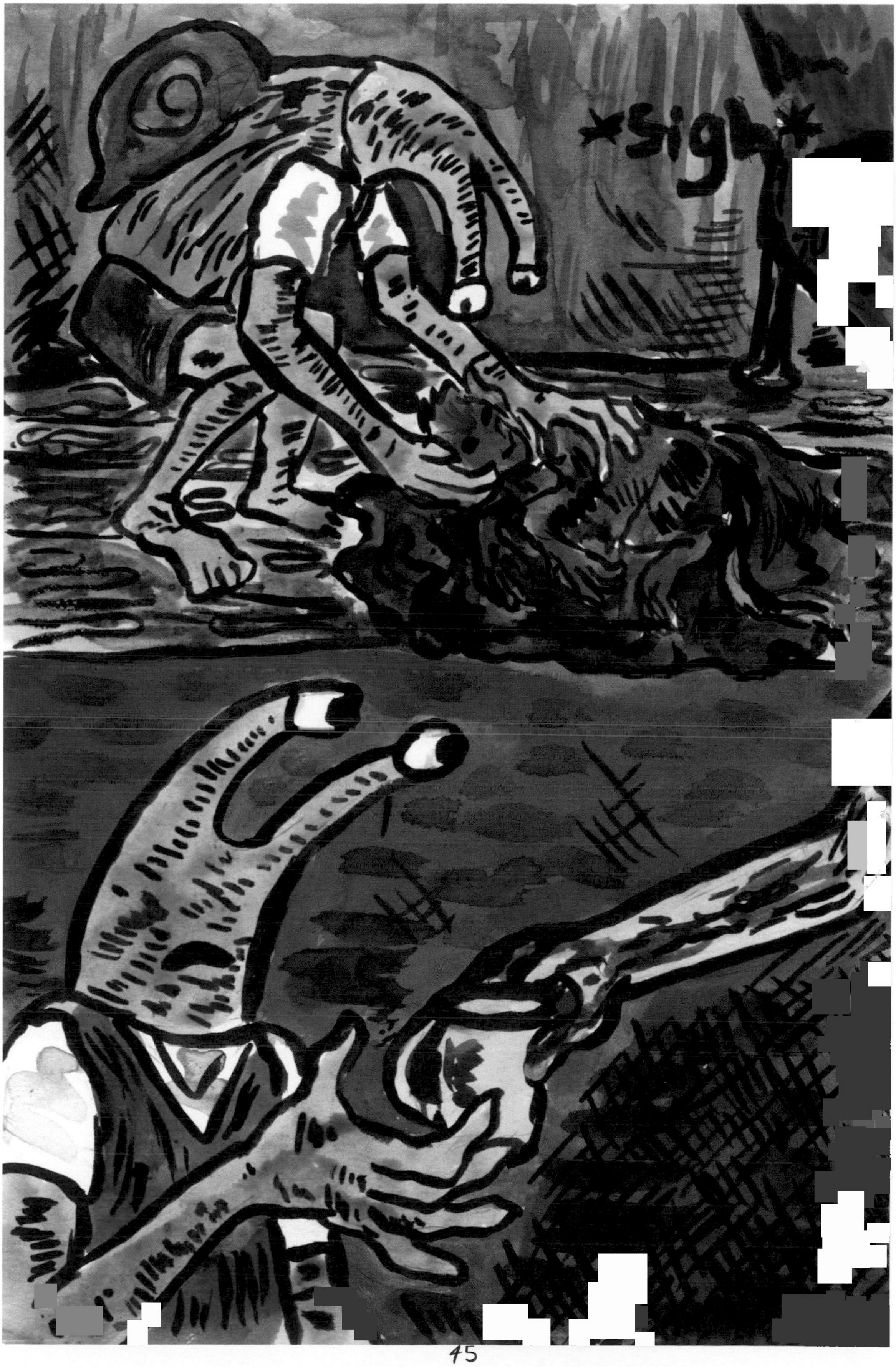
sigh

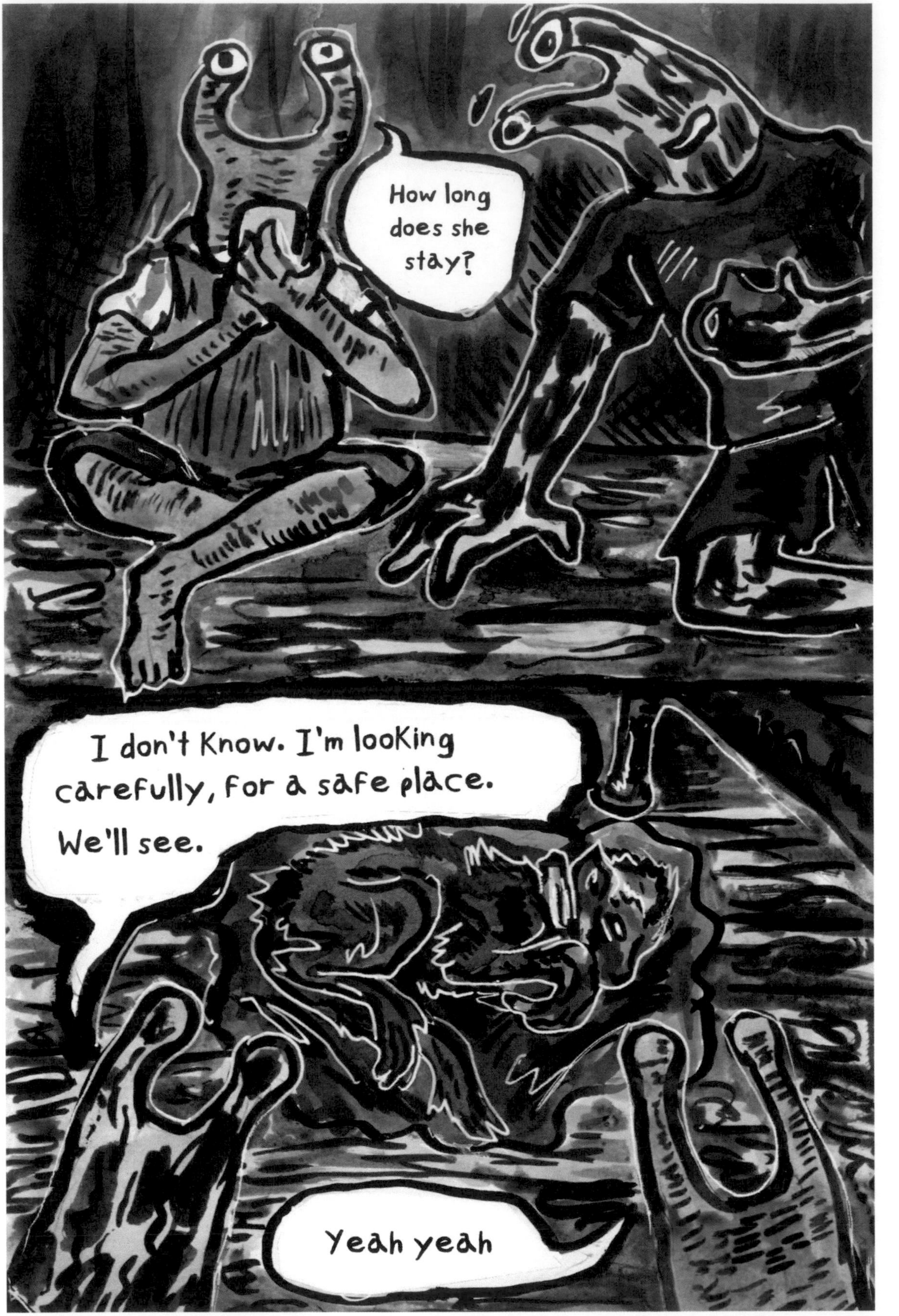
How long does she stay?
I don't Know. I'm looKing carefully, for a safe place. We'll see.
Yeah yeah

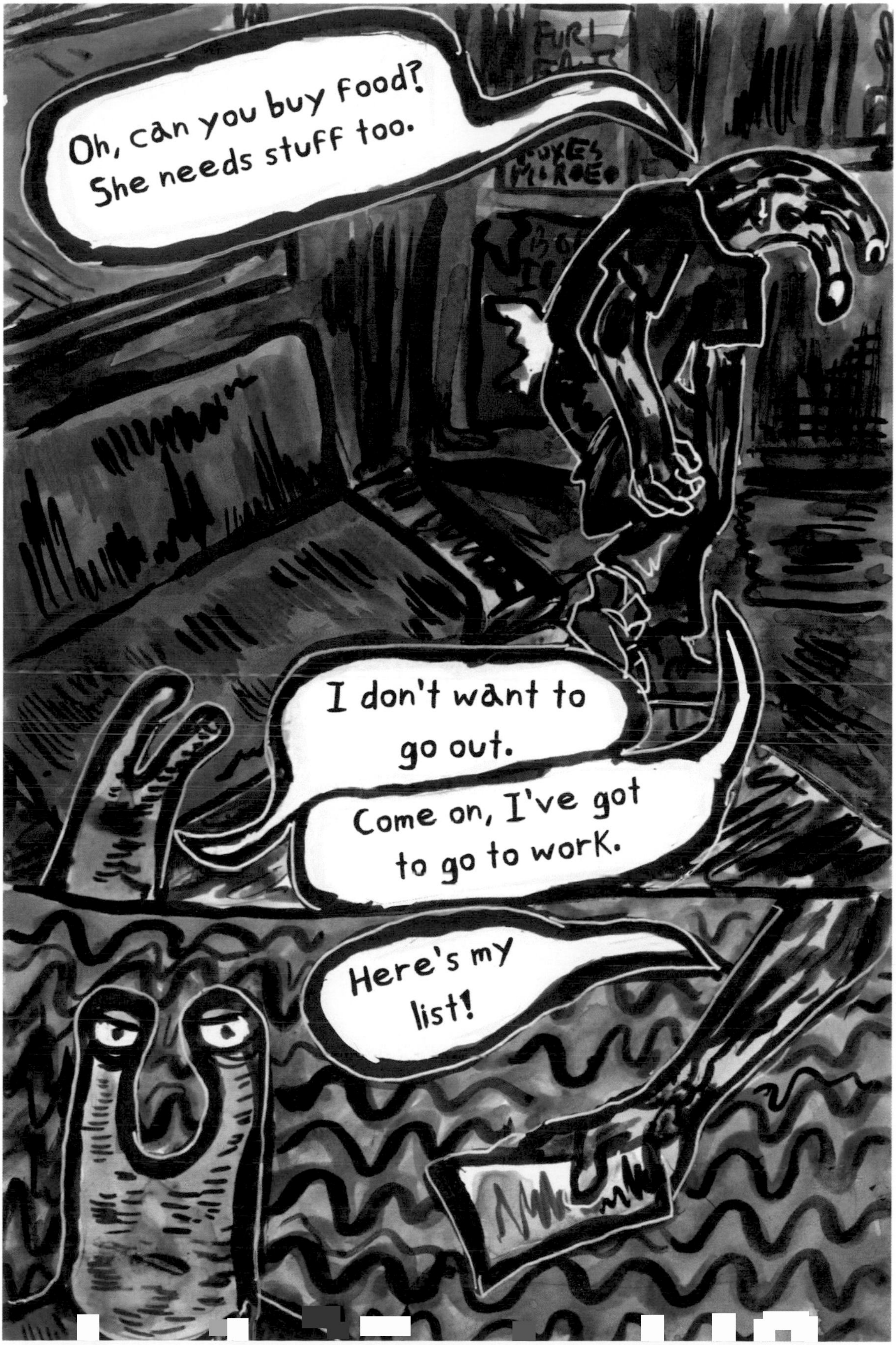
Oh, can you buy food? She needs stuff too.
I don't want to go out.
Come on, I've got to go to work.
Here's my list!

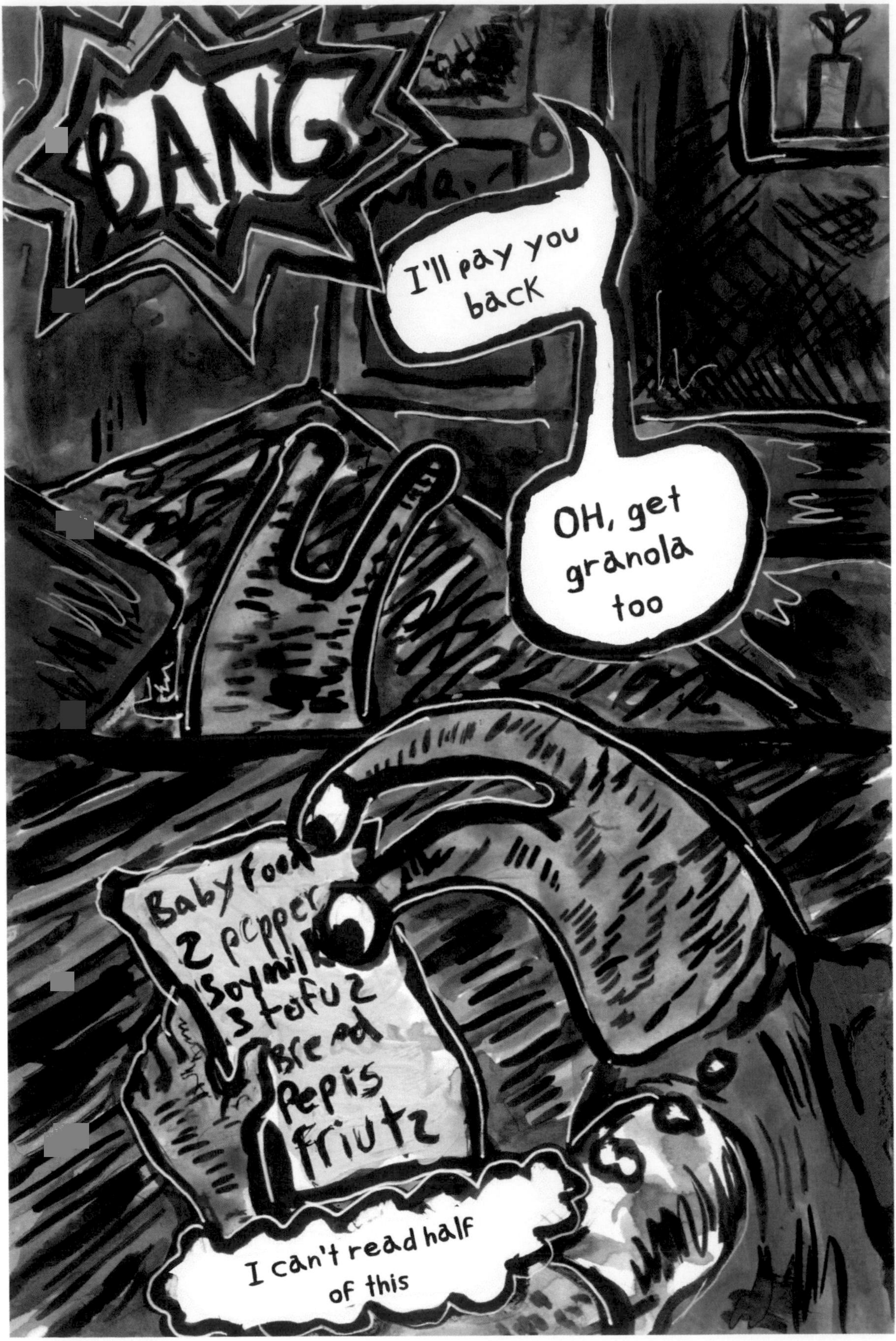
BANG!
I'll pay you back
OH, get granola too
Baby Foo
2 pepper
Soymil
3 tofu2
Bread
Pepis
friutz
I can't read half of this

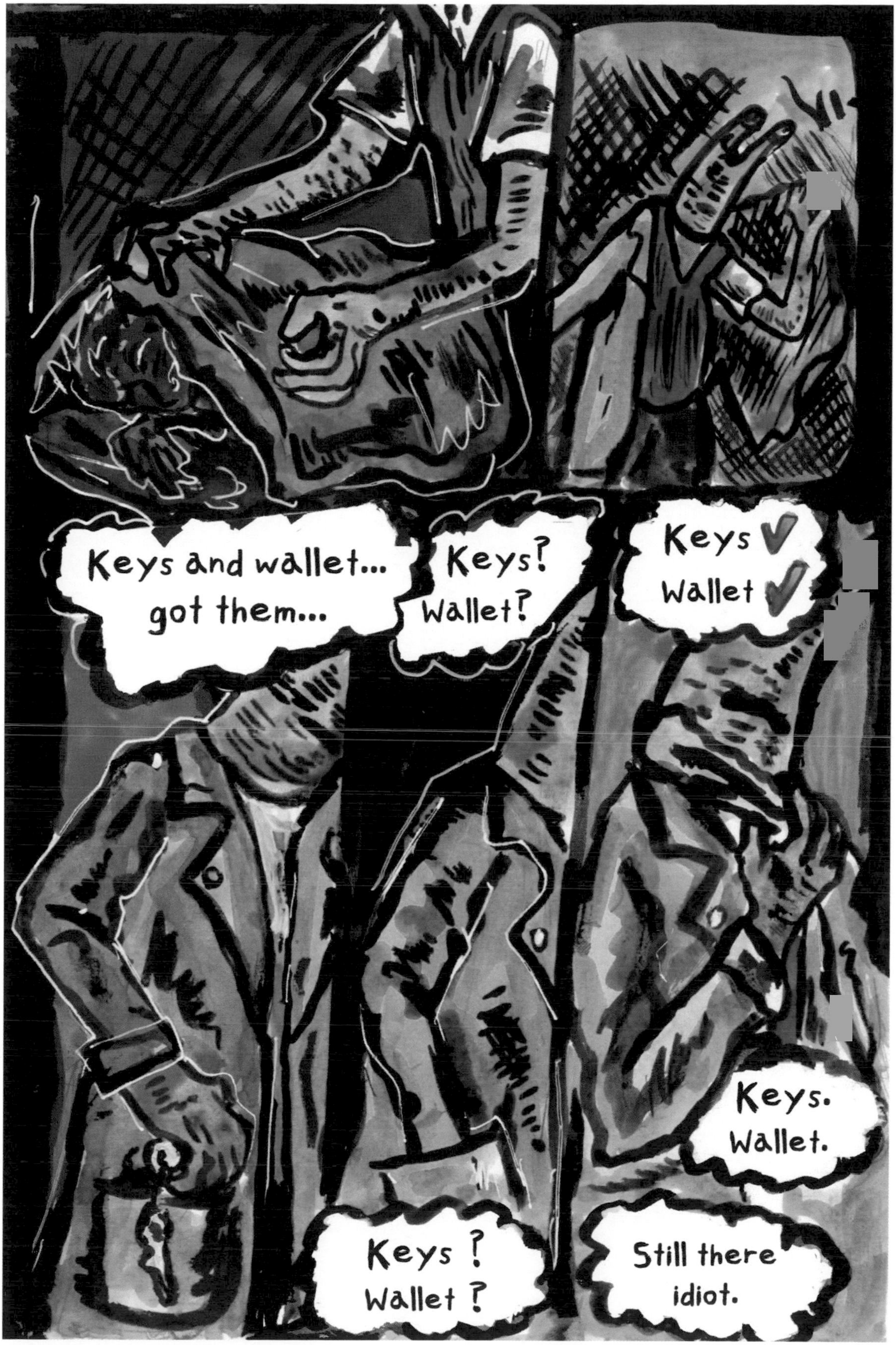
Keys and wallet... got them...
Keys? Wallet?
Keys ✓ Wallet ✓
Keys. Wallet.
Keys ? Wallet ?
Still there idiot.

Those people are looking at me. They Know about the monKey.
FREE DIVORCE CLAS
I'm gonna come home and that monKey will have hung herself.
Boyd isn't paying me back. That's fair I earned that.
I'll have explain to Boyd why she's dead.

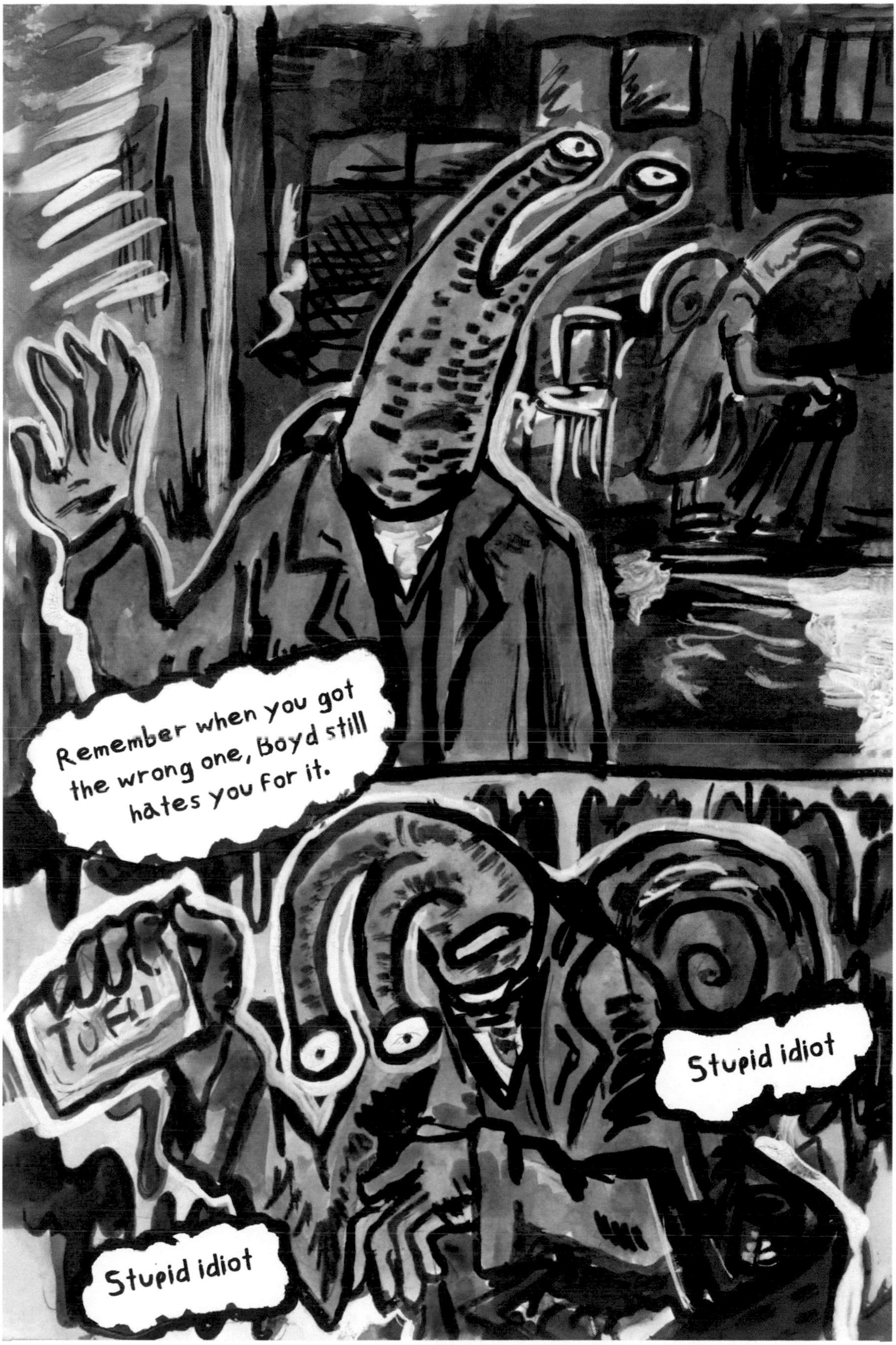
Remember when you got the wrong one, Boyd still hates you for it.
TOFU
Stupid idiot
Stupid idiot

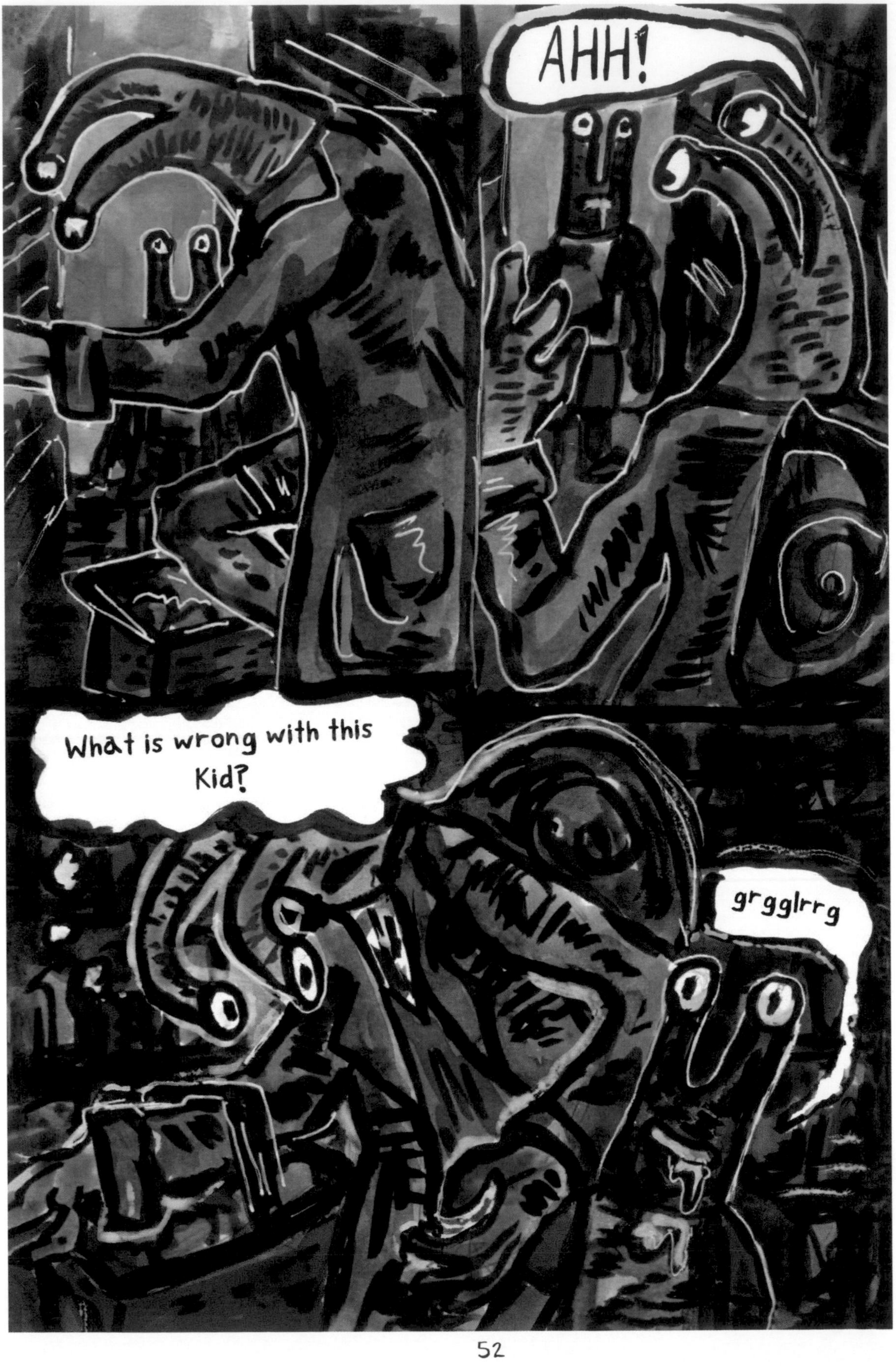
AHH!
What is wrong with this Kid?
grgglrrg

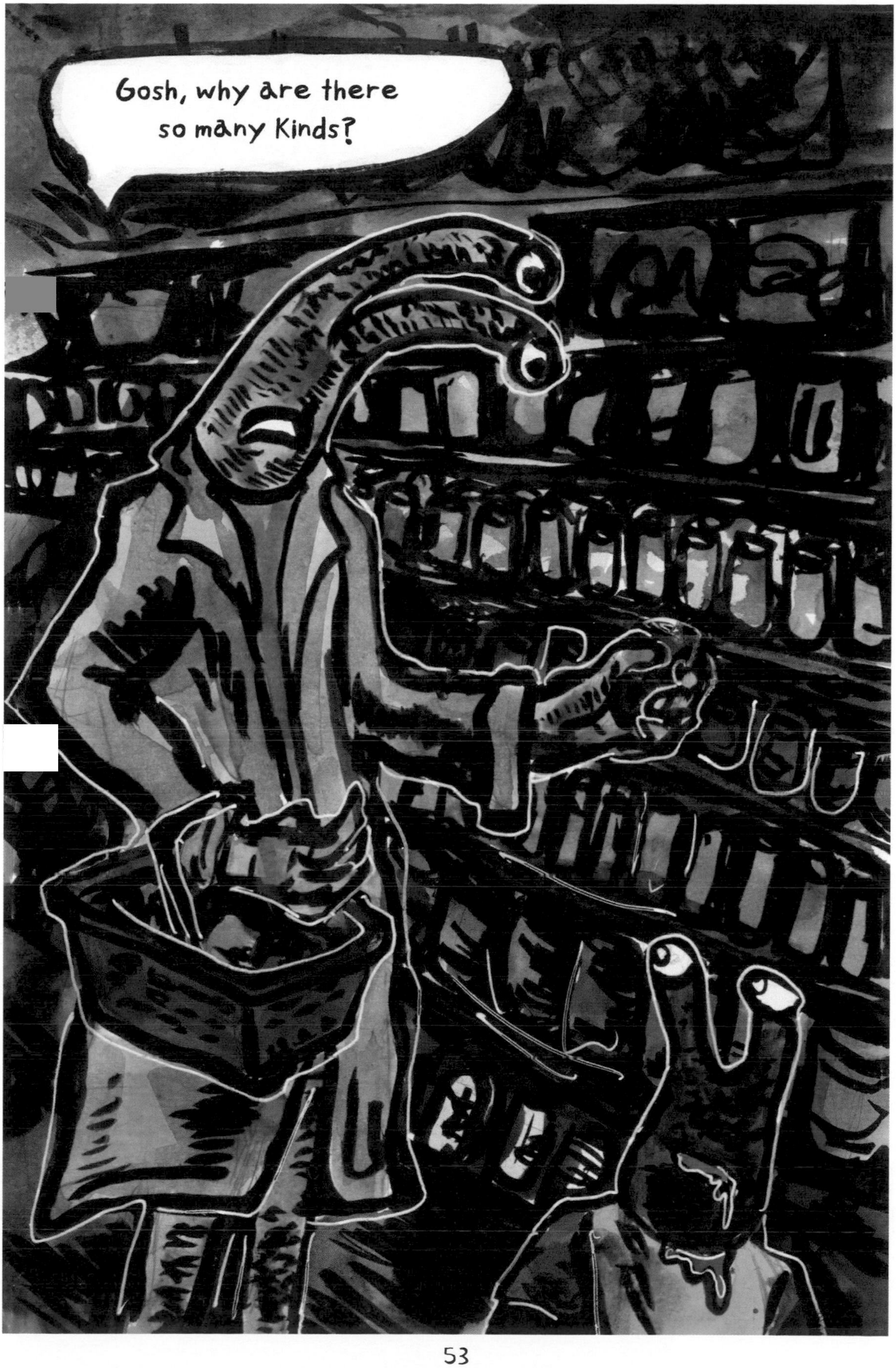
Gosh, why are there so many Kinds?

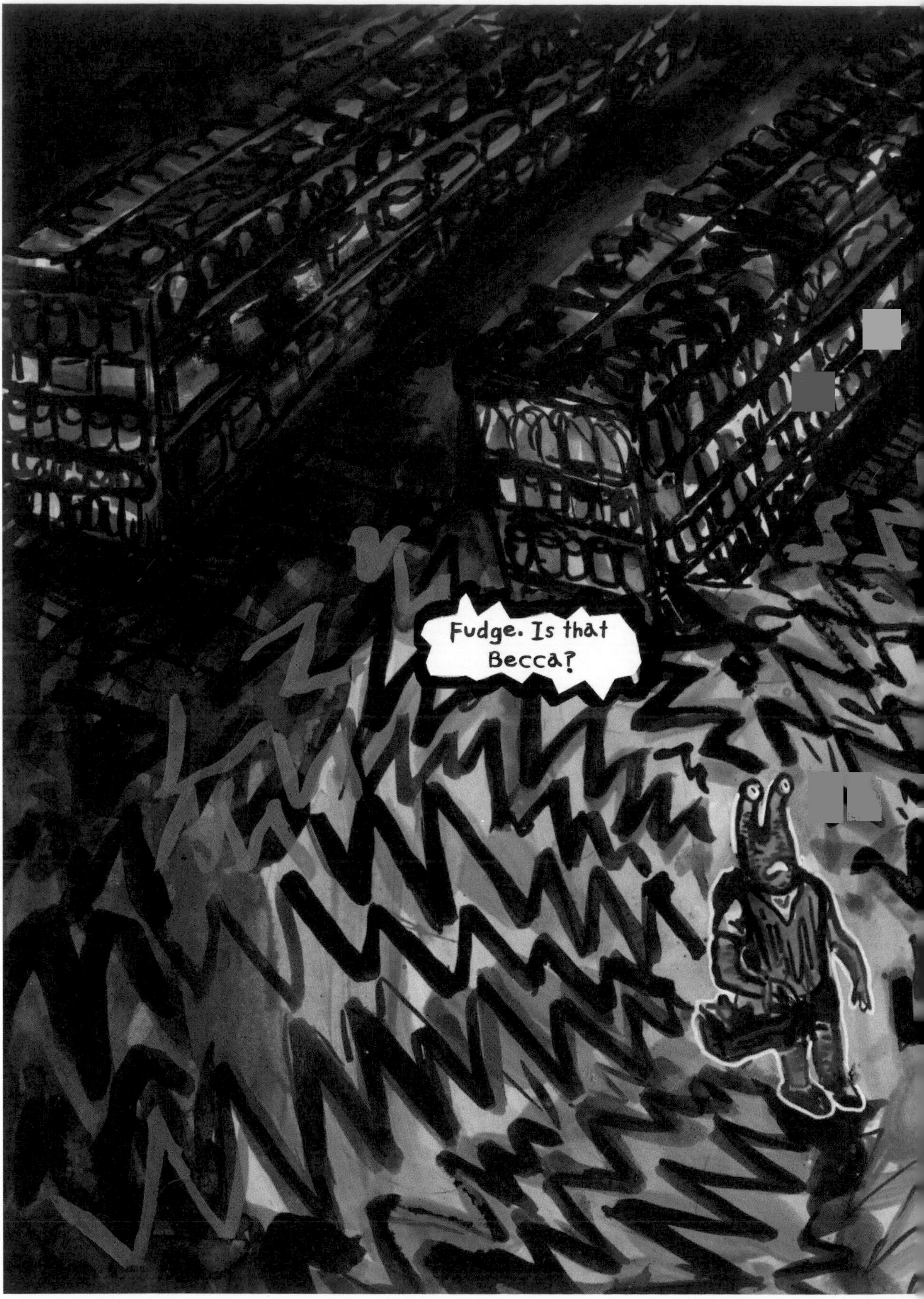
Fudge. Is that Becca?

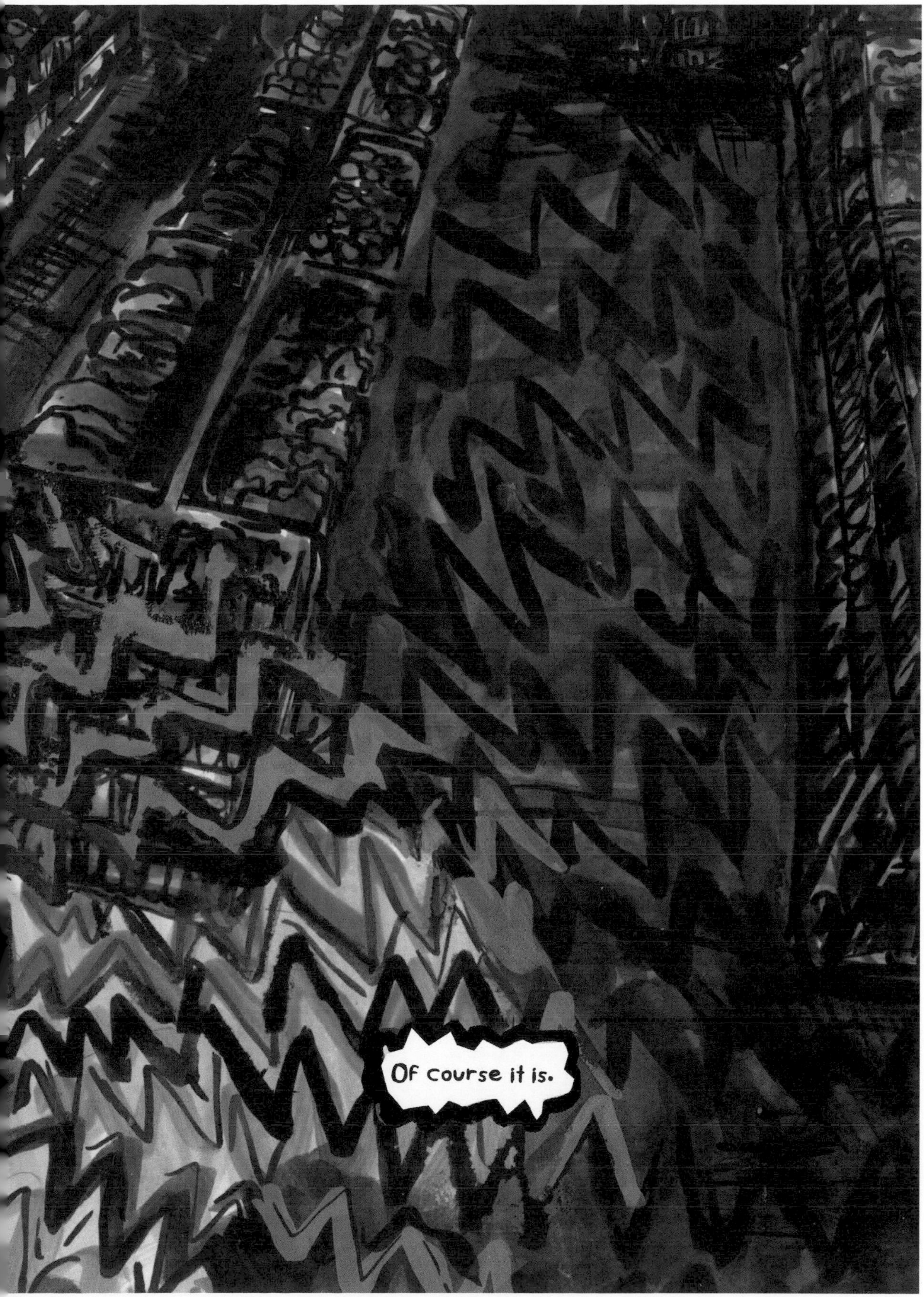
Of course it is.

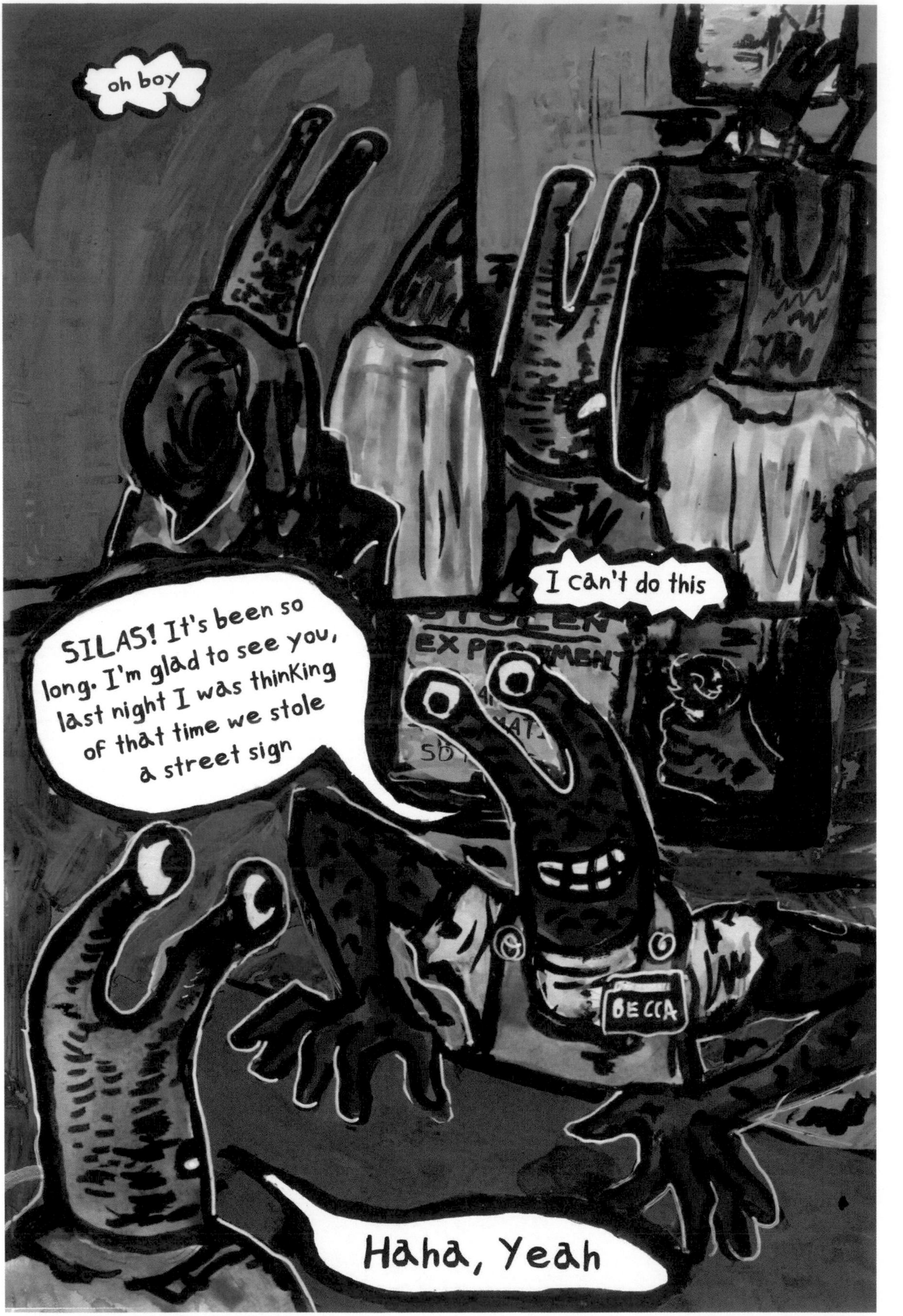
oh boy
I can't do this
SILAS! It's been so long. I'm glad to see you, last night I was thinking of that time we stole a street sign
BECCA
Haha, Yeah

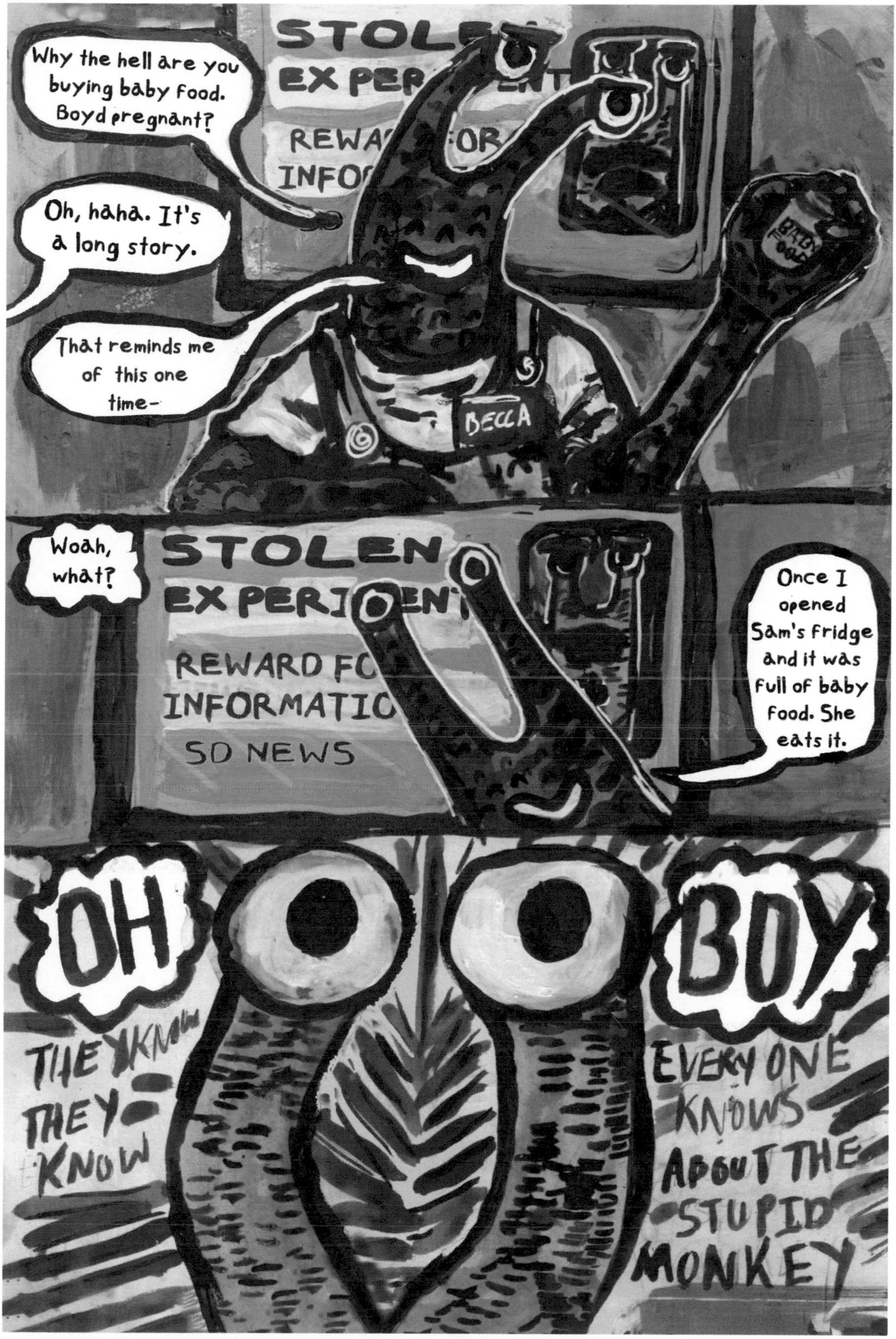

Why the hell are you buying baby food. Boyd pregnant?
Oh, haha. It's a long story.
That reminds me of this one time-
STOLEN EXPERIMENT
REWARD FOR INFORMATION
SD NEWS
BABY FOOD
BECCA
Woah, what?
Once I opened Sam's fridge and it was full of baby food. She eats it.
OH BOY
THEY KNOW THEY KNOW
EVERY ONE KNOWS ABOUT THE STUPID MONKEY

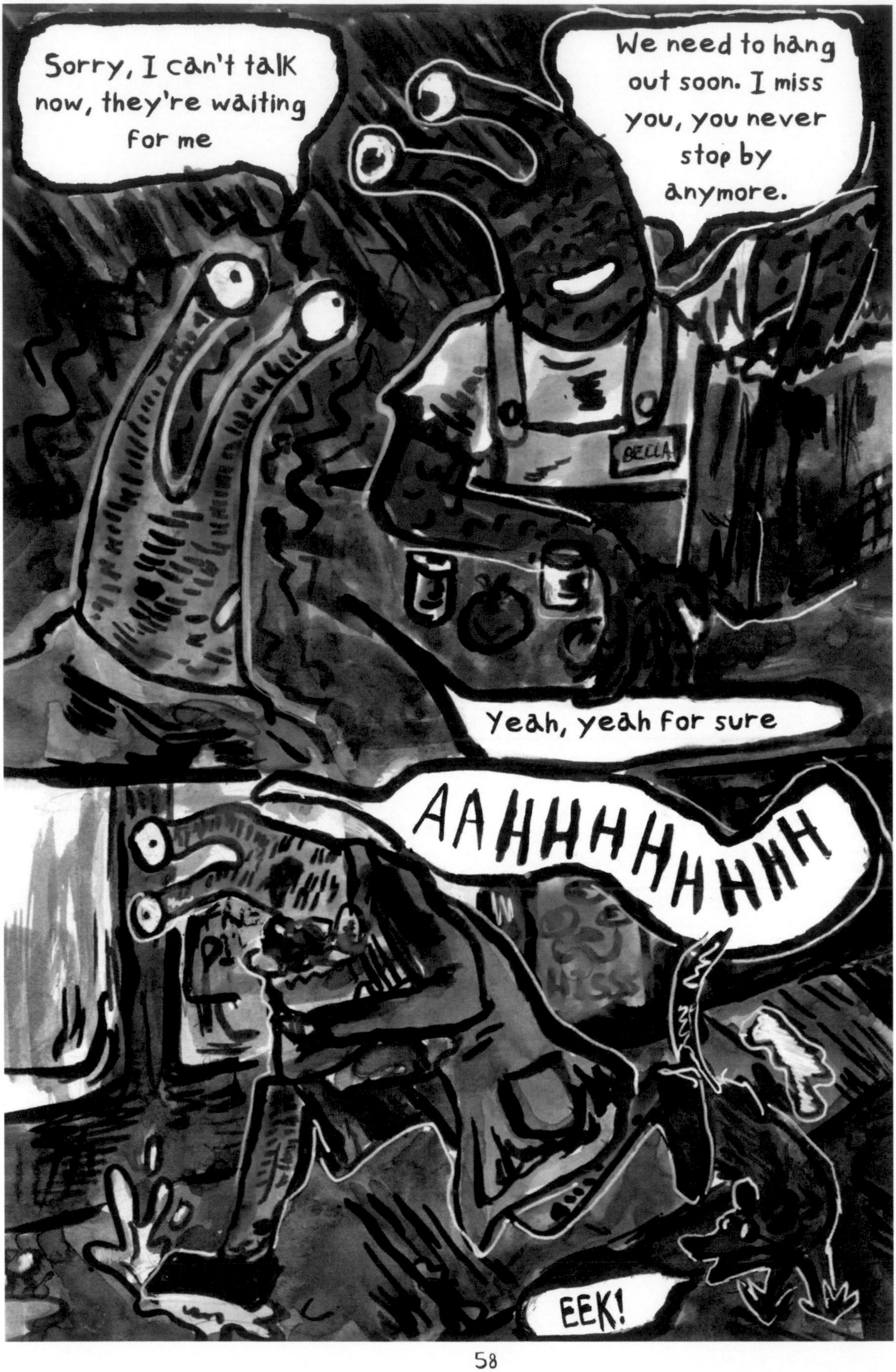
Sorry, I can't talk now, they're waiting for me
We need to hang out soon. I miss you, you never stop by anymore.
BELLA
Yeah, yeah for sure
AAHHHHHHHH
EEK!

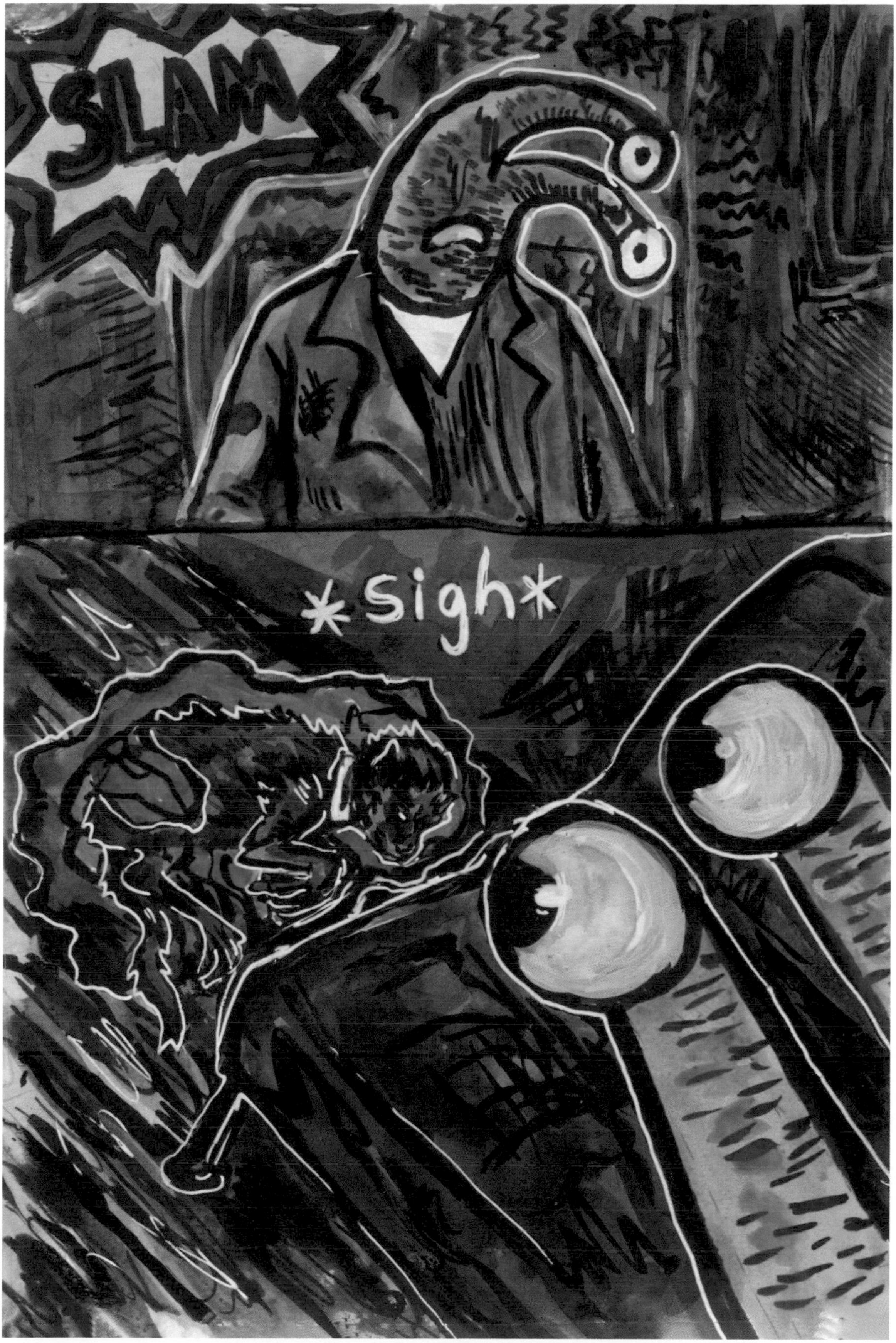
SLAM
sigh

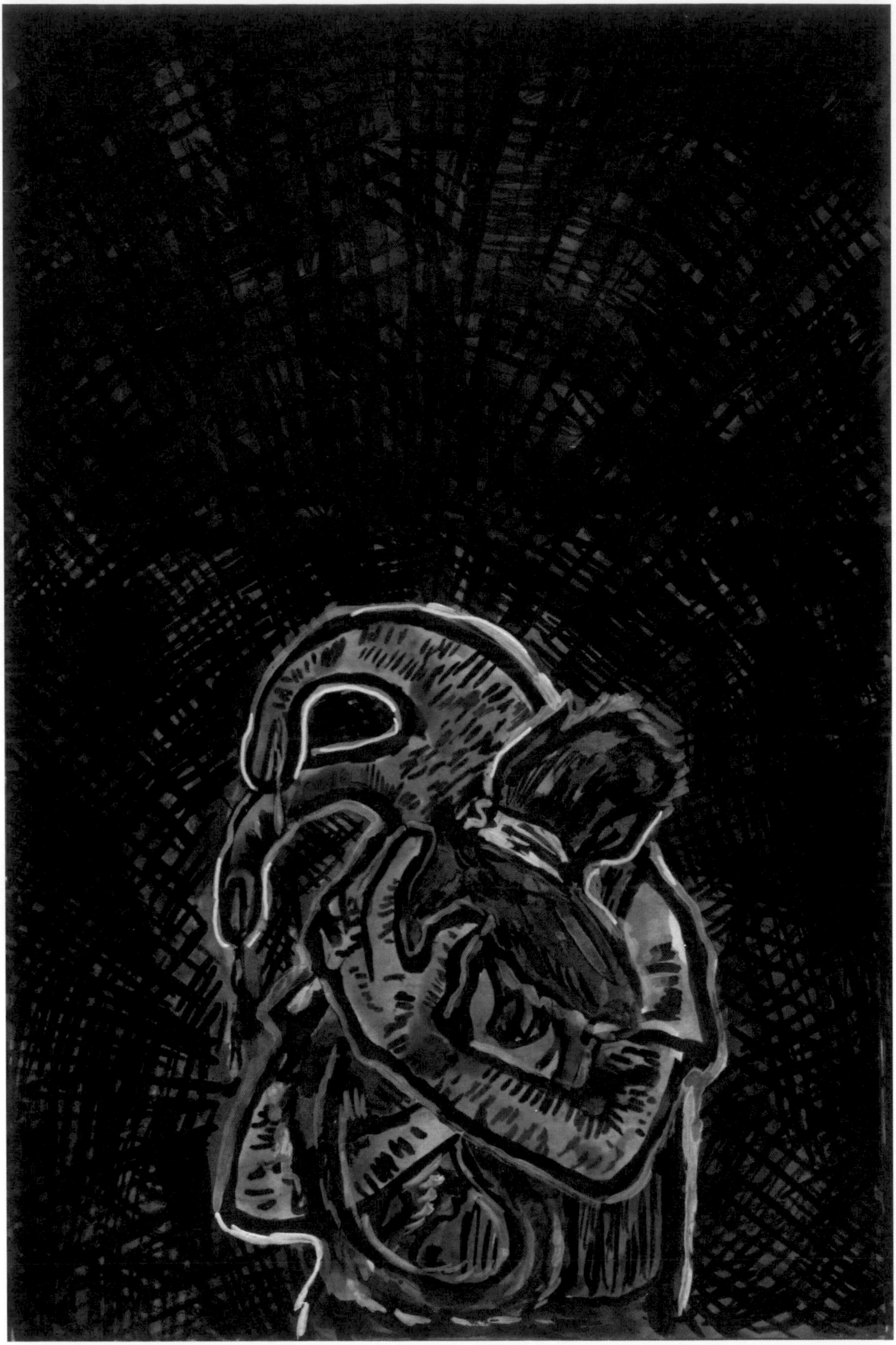

CHAPTER 4

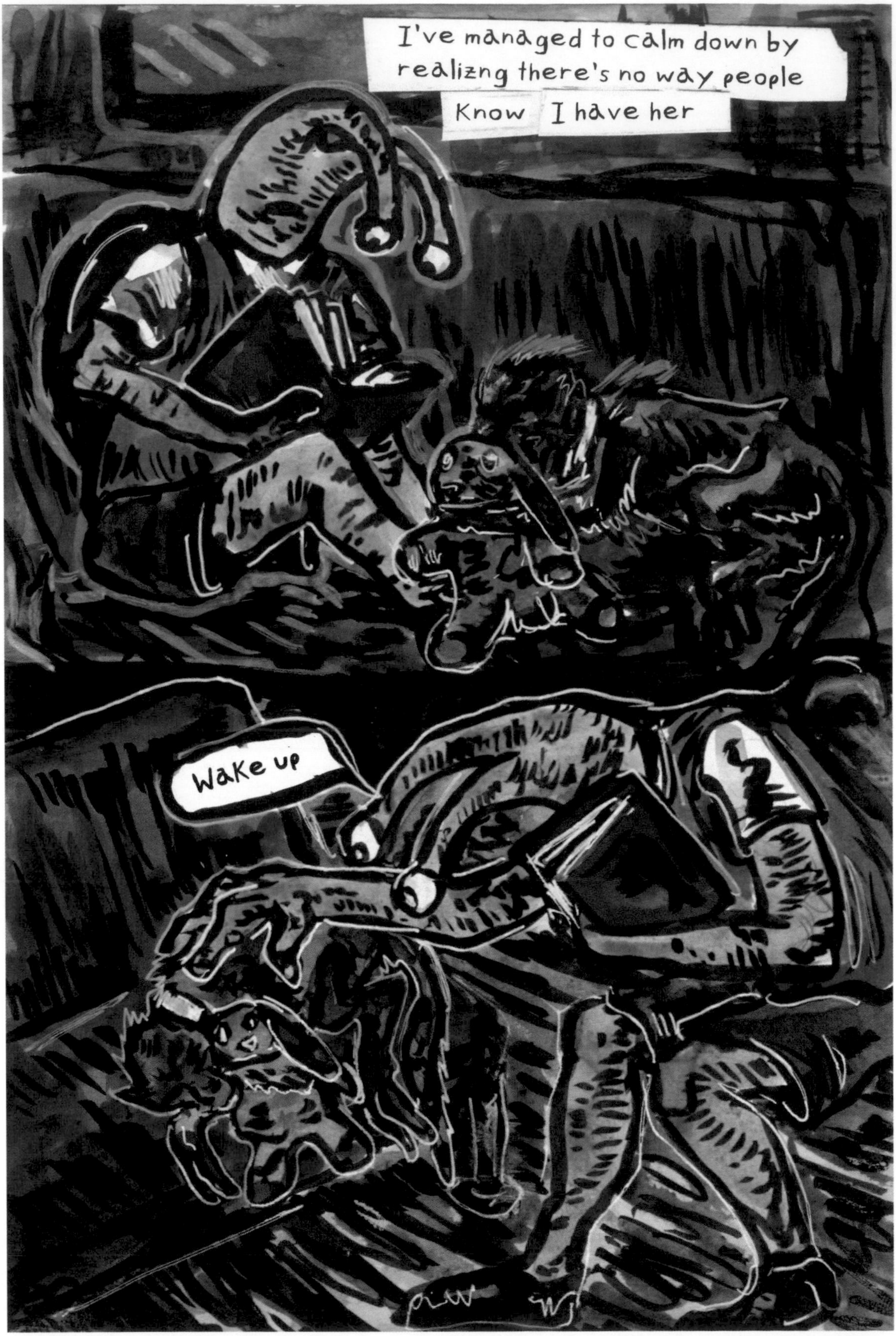
I've managed to calm down by realizng there's no way people
Know
I have her
Wake up

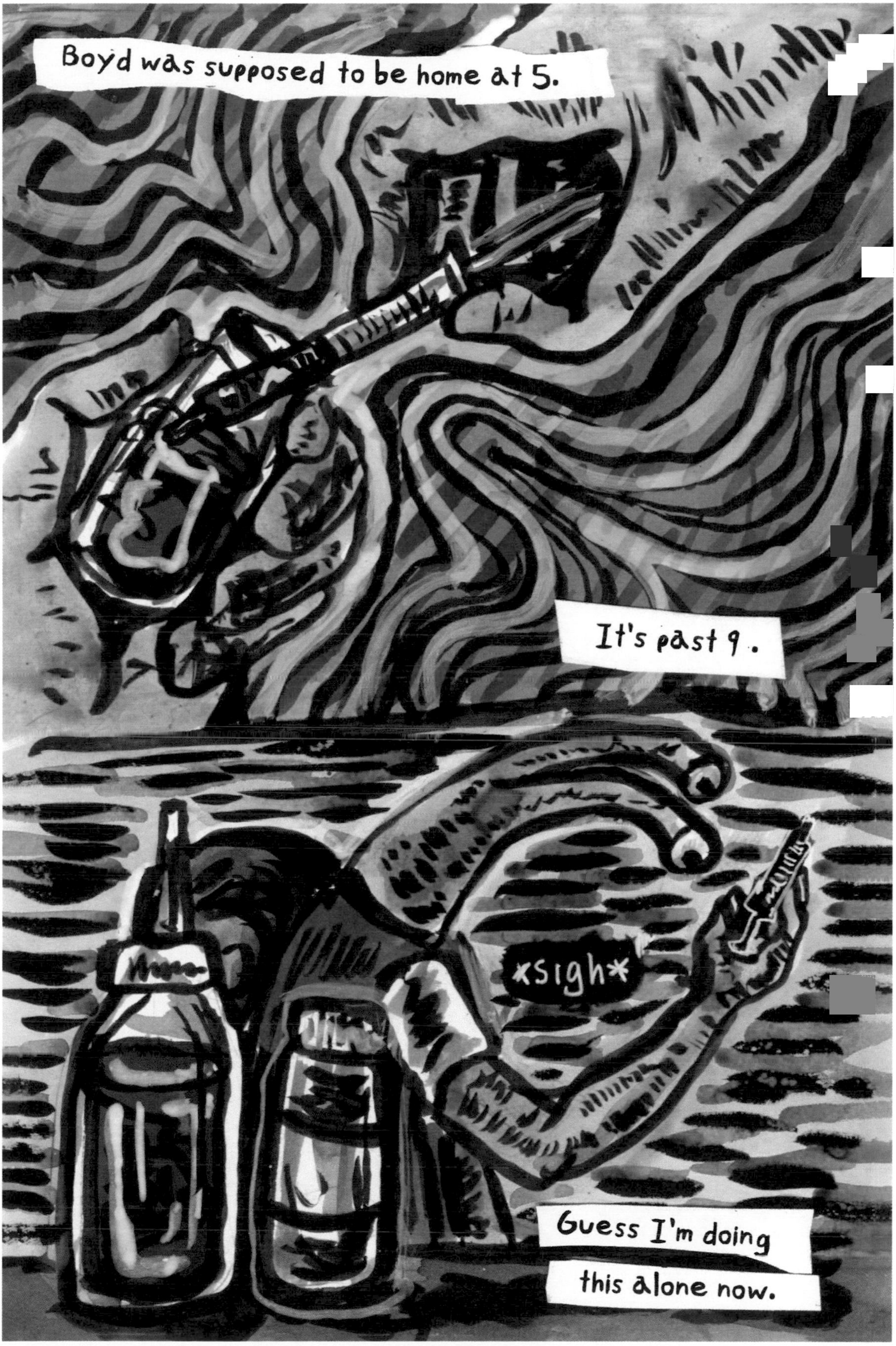
Boyd was supposed to be home at 5.
It's past 9.
sigh
Guess I'm doing
this alone now.

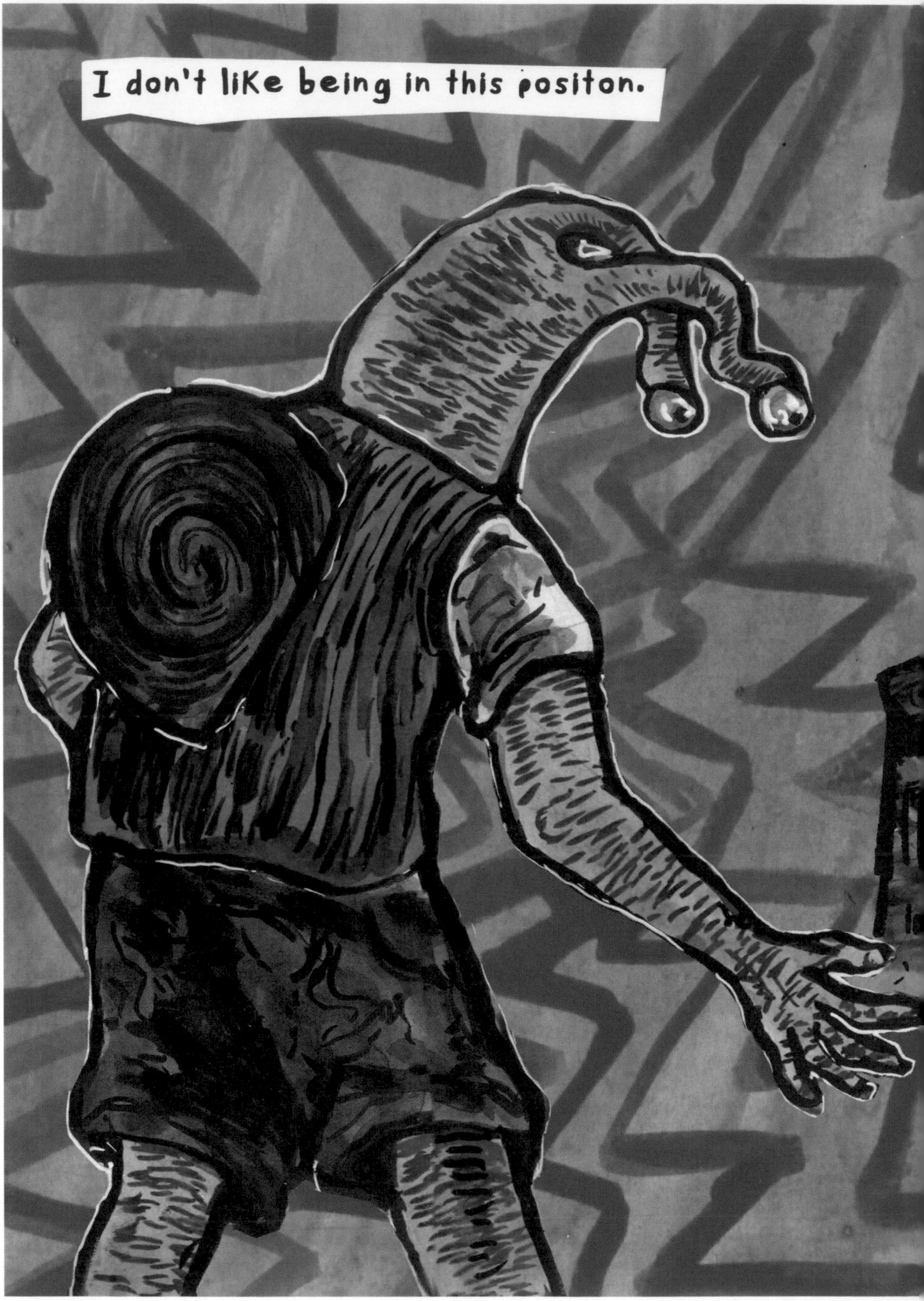
I don't like being in this positon.

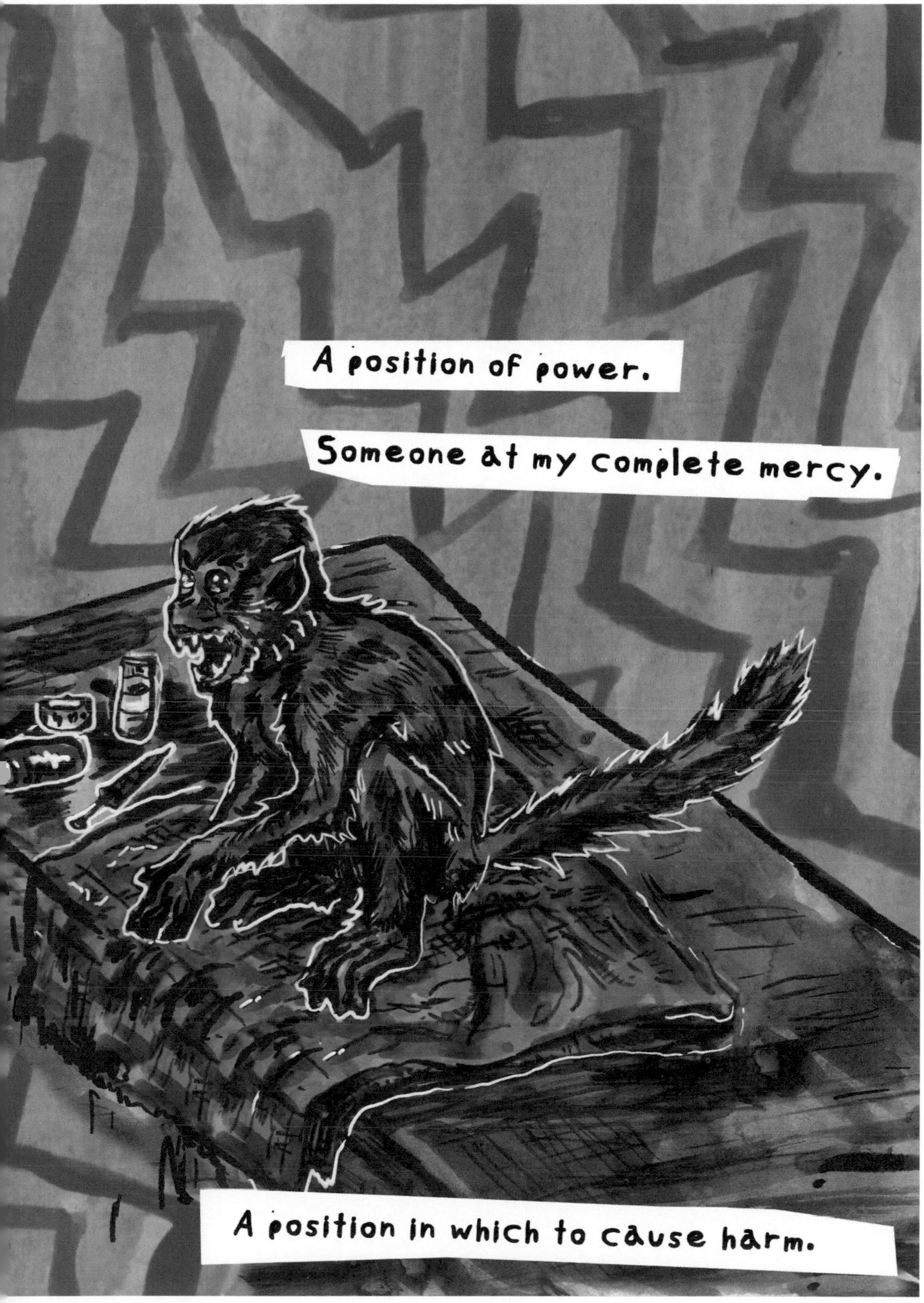
A position of power.
Someone at my complete mercy.
A position in which to cause harm.

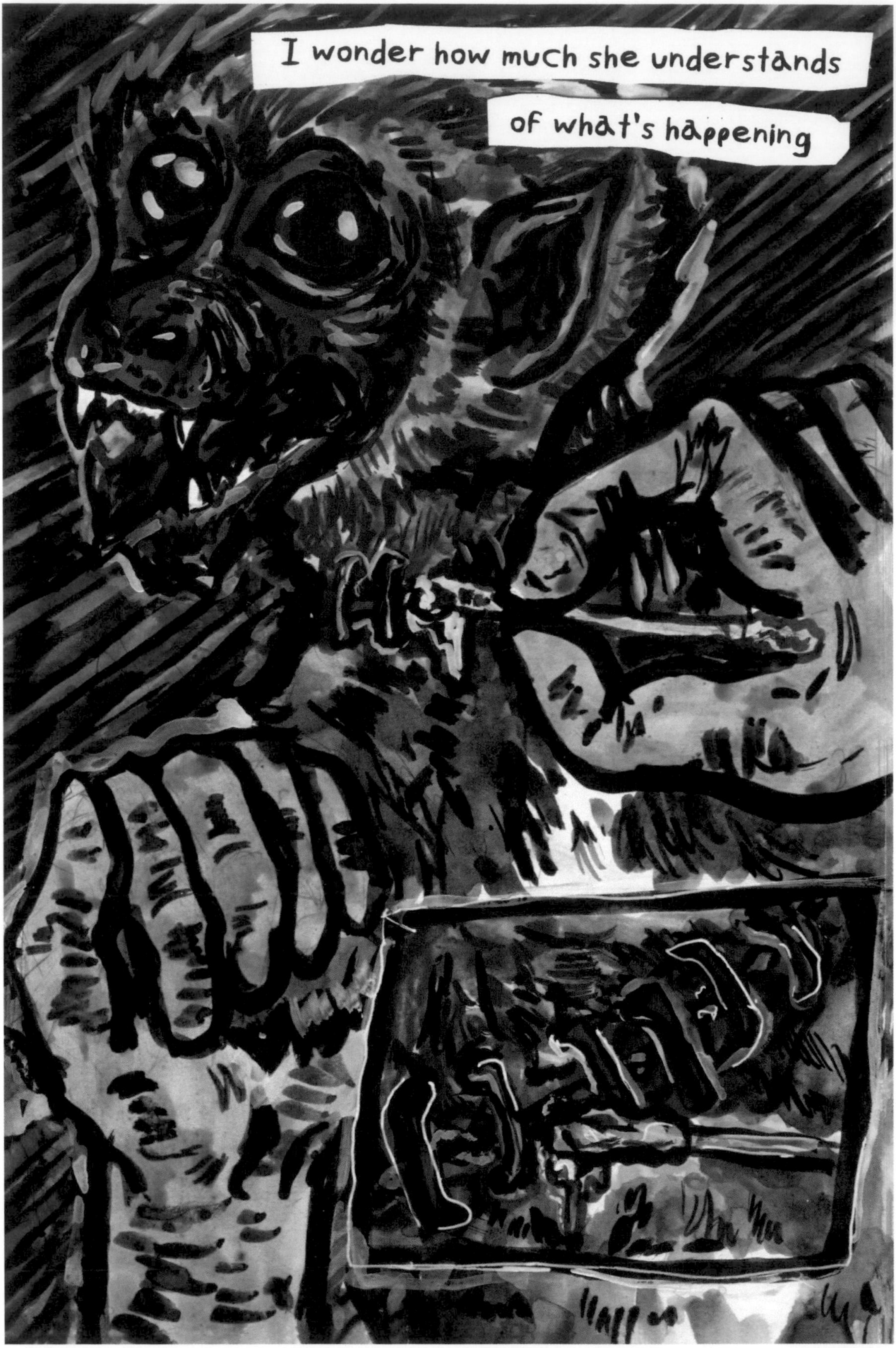
I wonder how much she understands
of what's happening

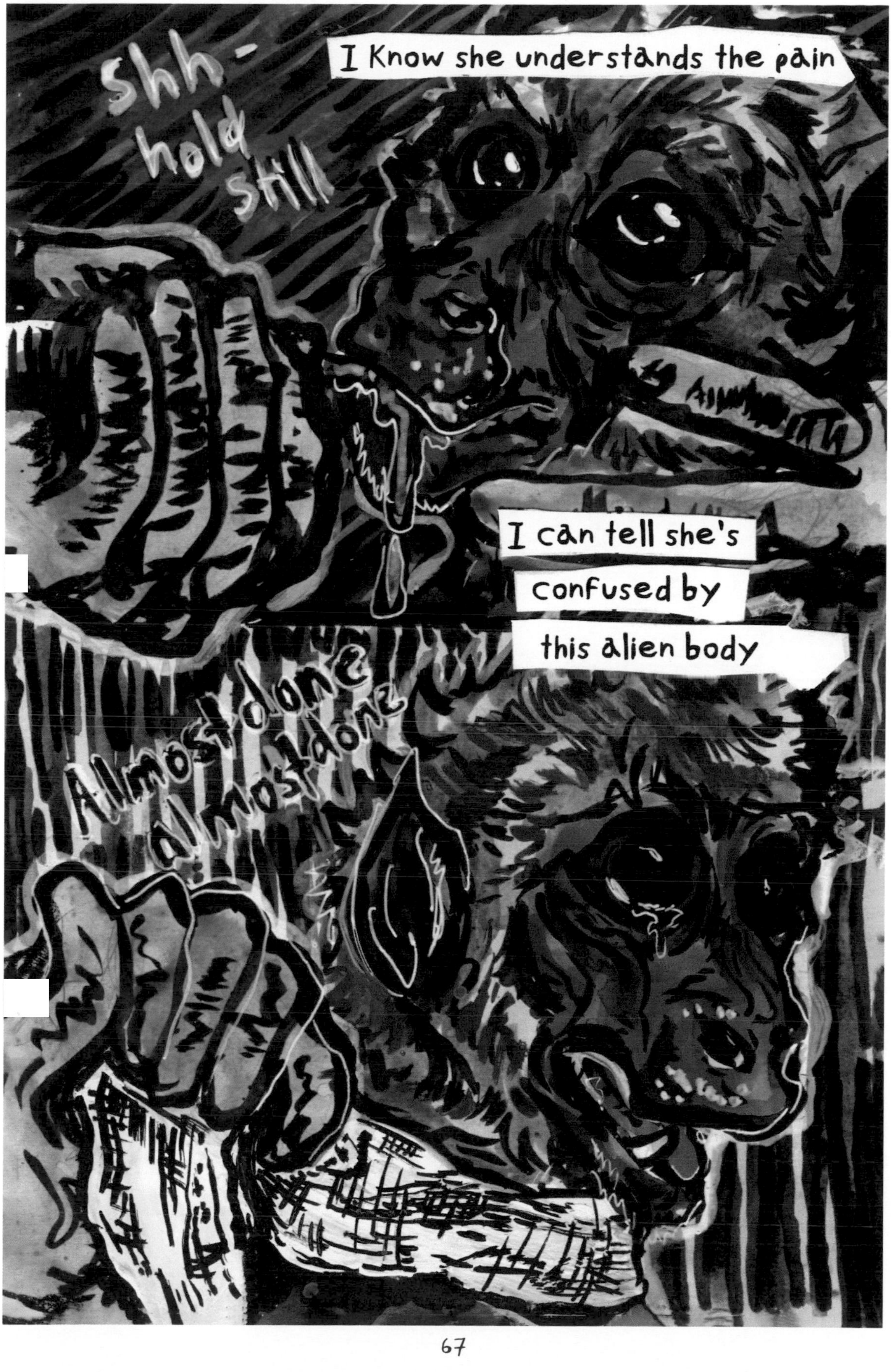
Shh-
hold
still
I Know she understands the pain
I can tell she's
confused by
this alien body
Almost done
almost done

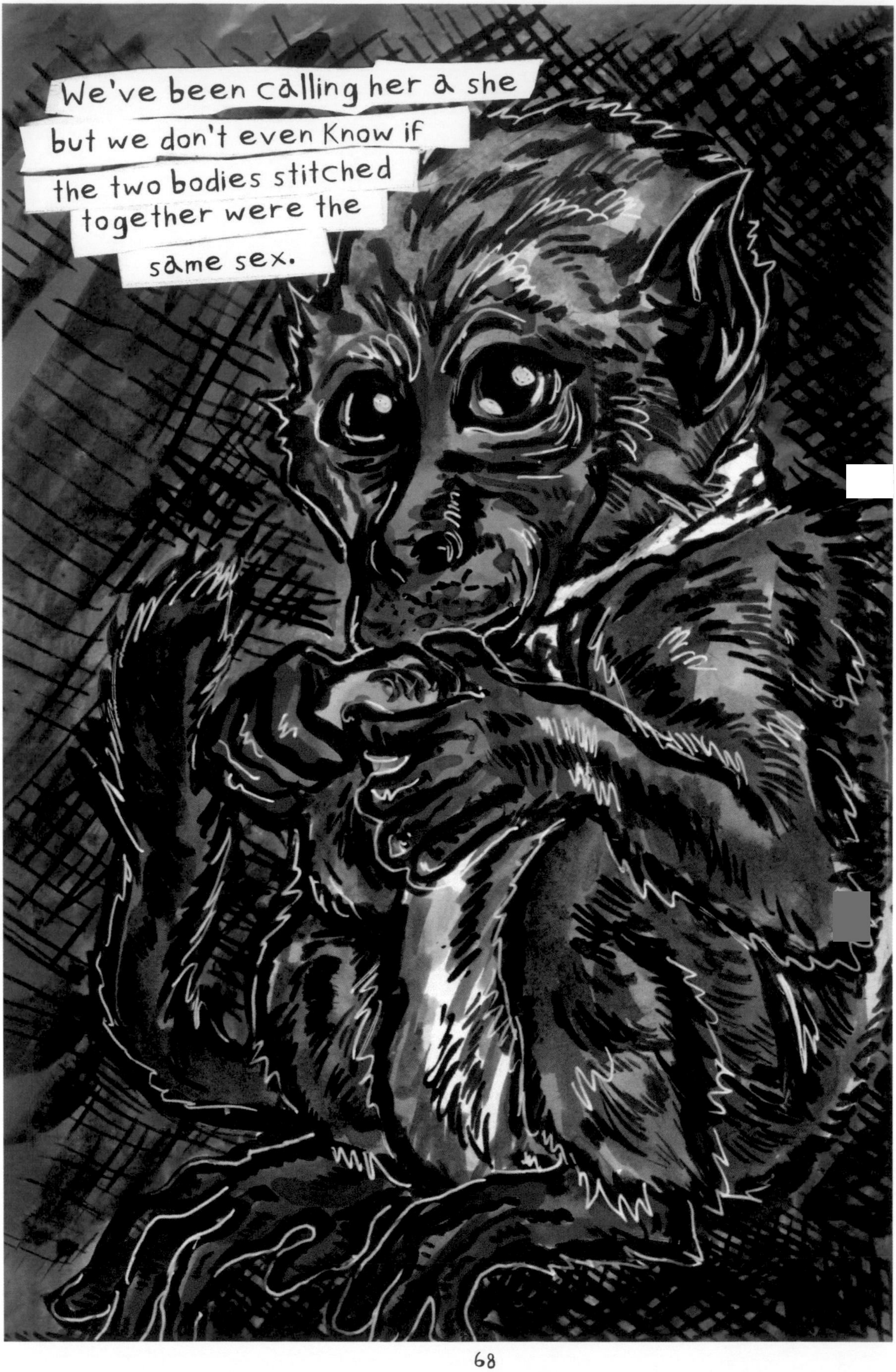
We've been calling her a she
but we don't even Know if
the two bodies stitched
together were the
same sex.

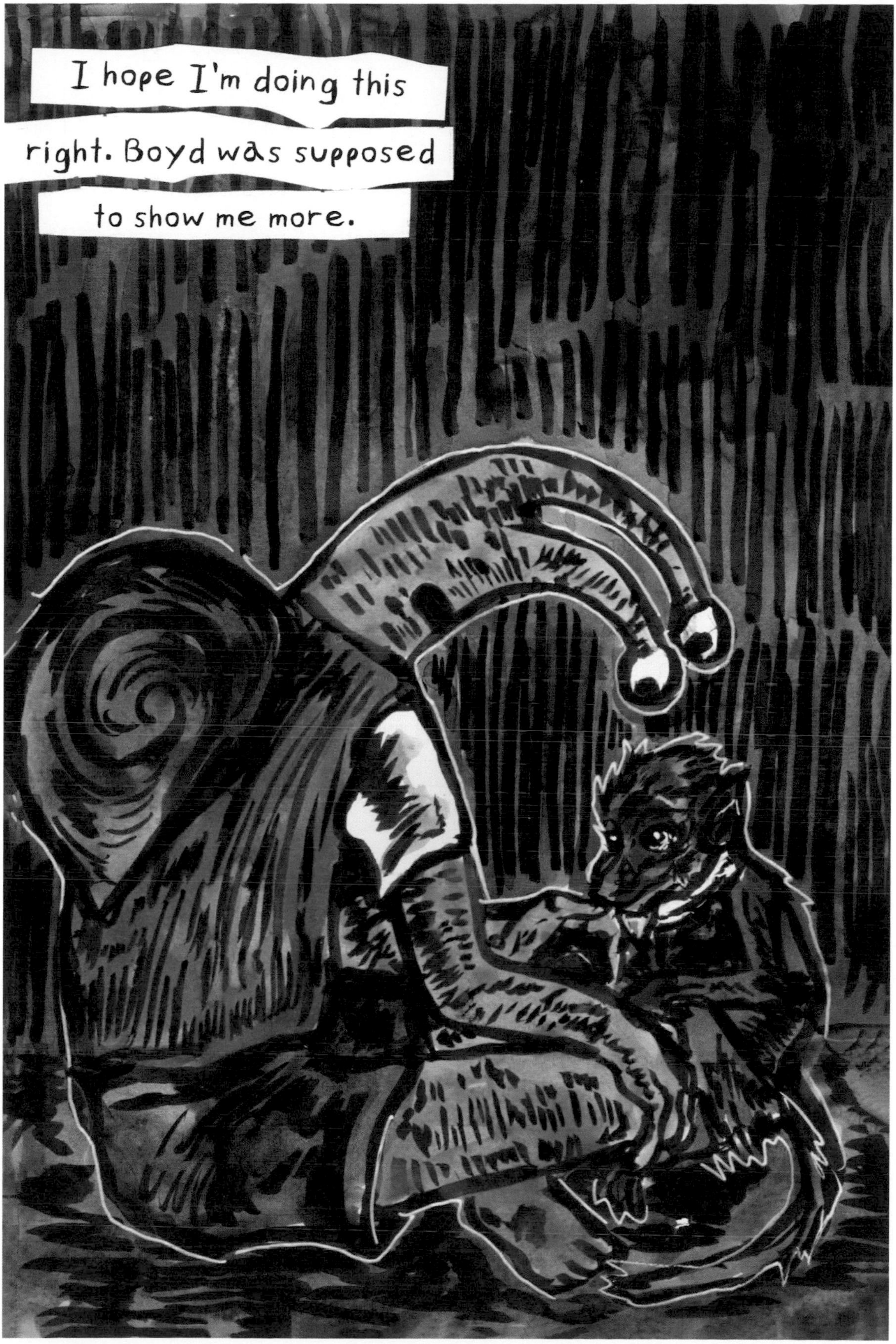
I hope I'm doing this
right. Boyd was supposed
to show me more.

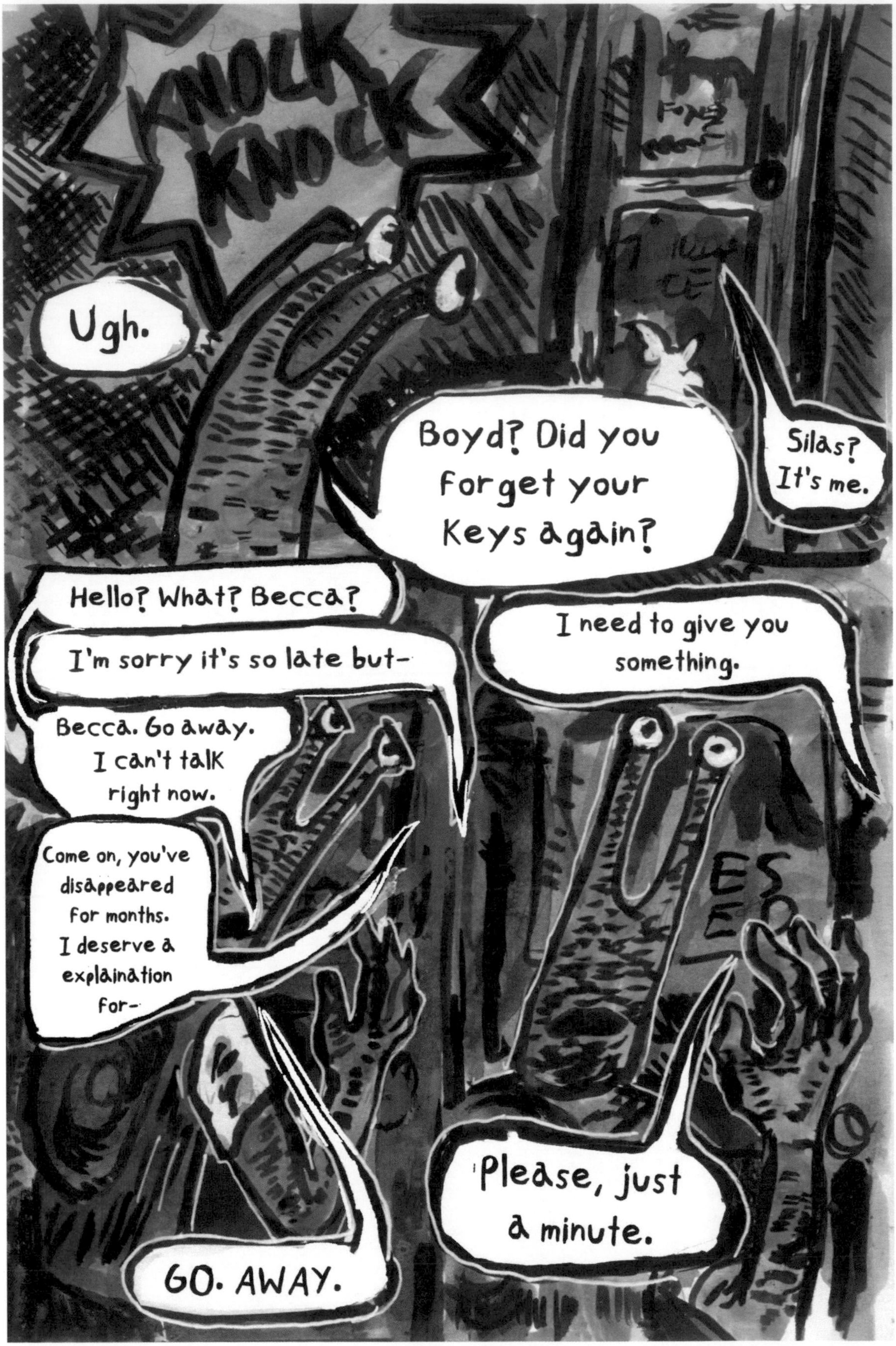
KNOCK KNOCK
Ugh.
Boyd? Did you forget your Keys again?
Silas? It's me.
Hello? What? Becca?
I'm sorry it's so late but-
I need to give you something.
Becca. Go away. I can't talk right now.
Come on, you've disappeared for months. I deserve a explaination for-
Please, just a minute.
GO. AWAY.

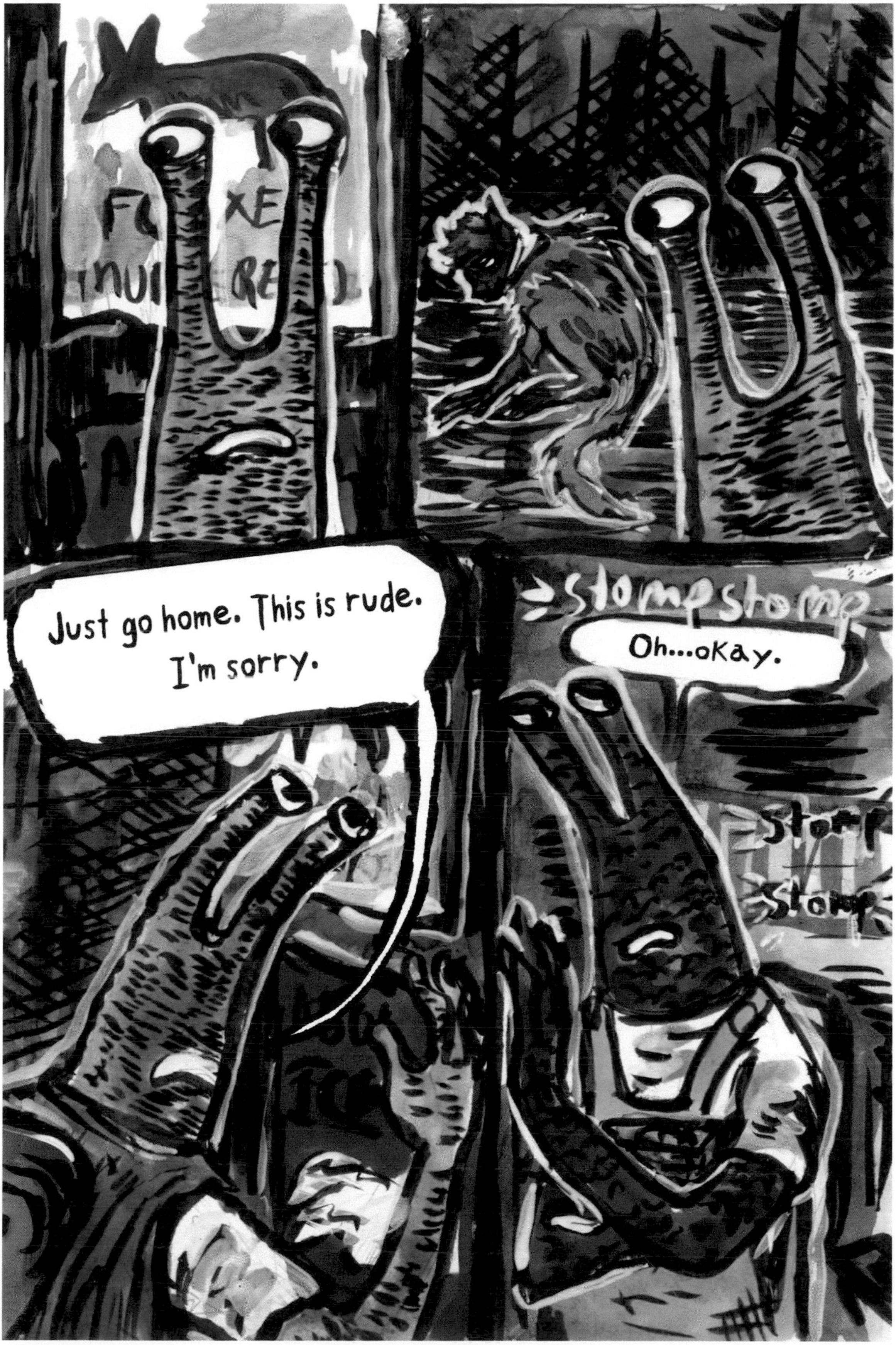
Just go home. This is rude. I'm sorry.
stomp stomp
Oh...okay.
stomp
stomp

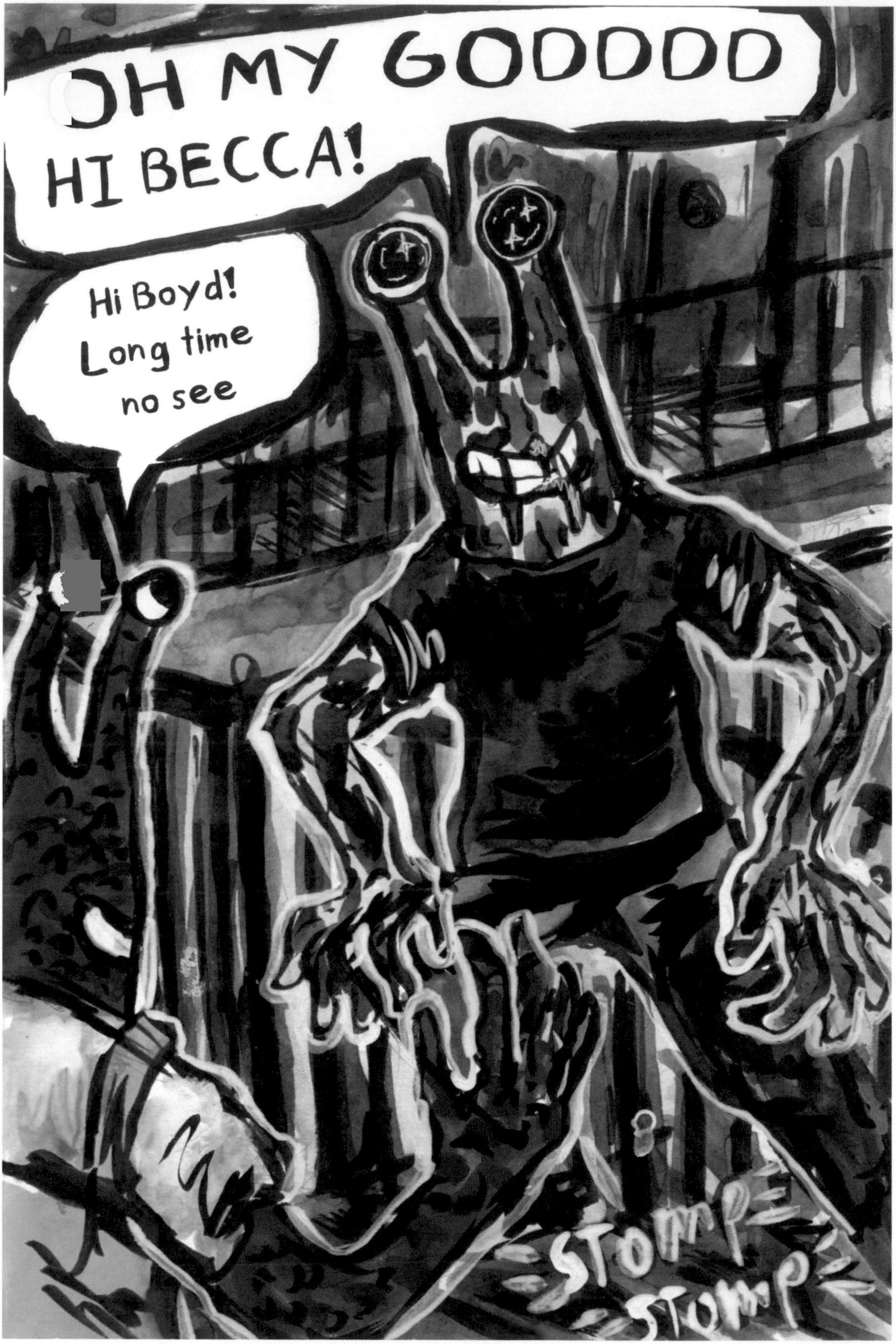
OH MY GODDDD
HI BECCA!
Hi Boyd! Long time no see
STOMP
STOMP

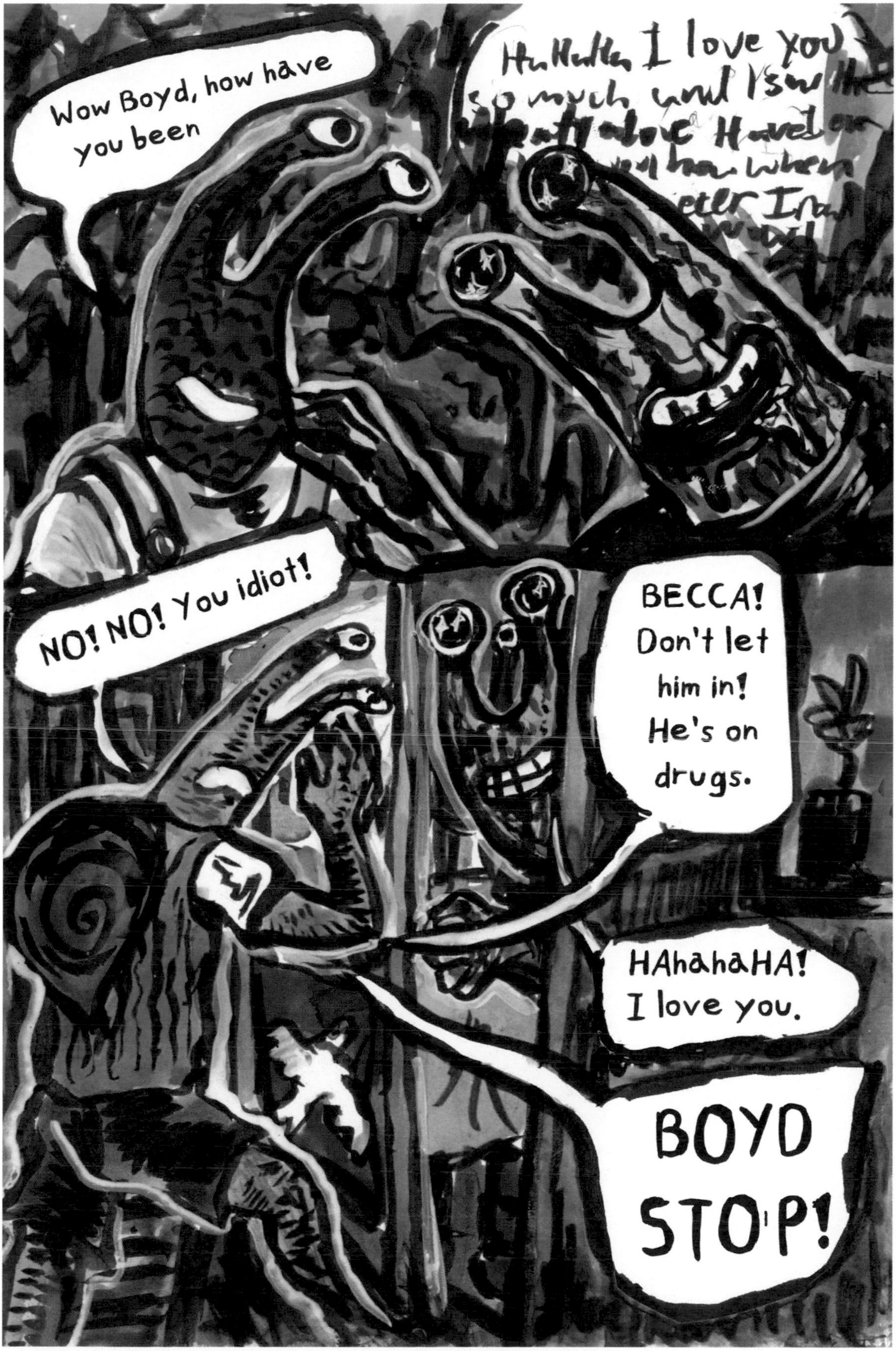
Wow Boyd, how have you been
I love you so much
NO! NO! You idiot!
BECCA! Don't let him in! He's on drugs.
HAhahaHA! I love you.
BOYD STOP!

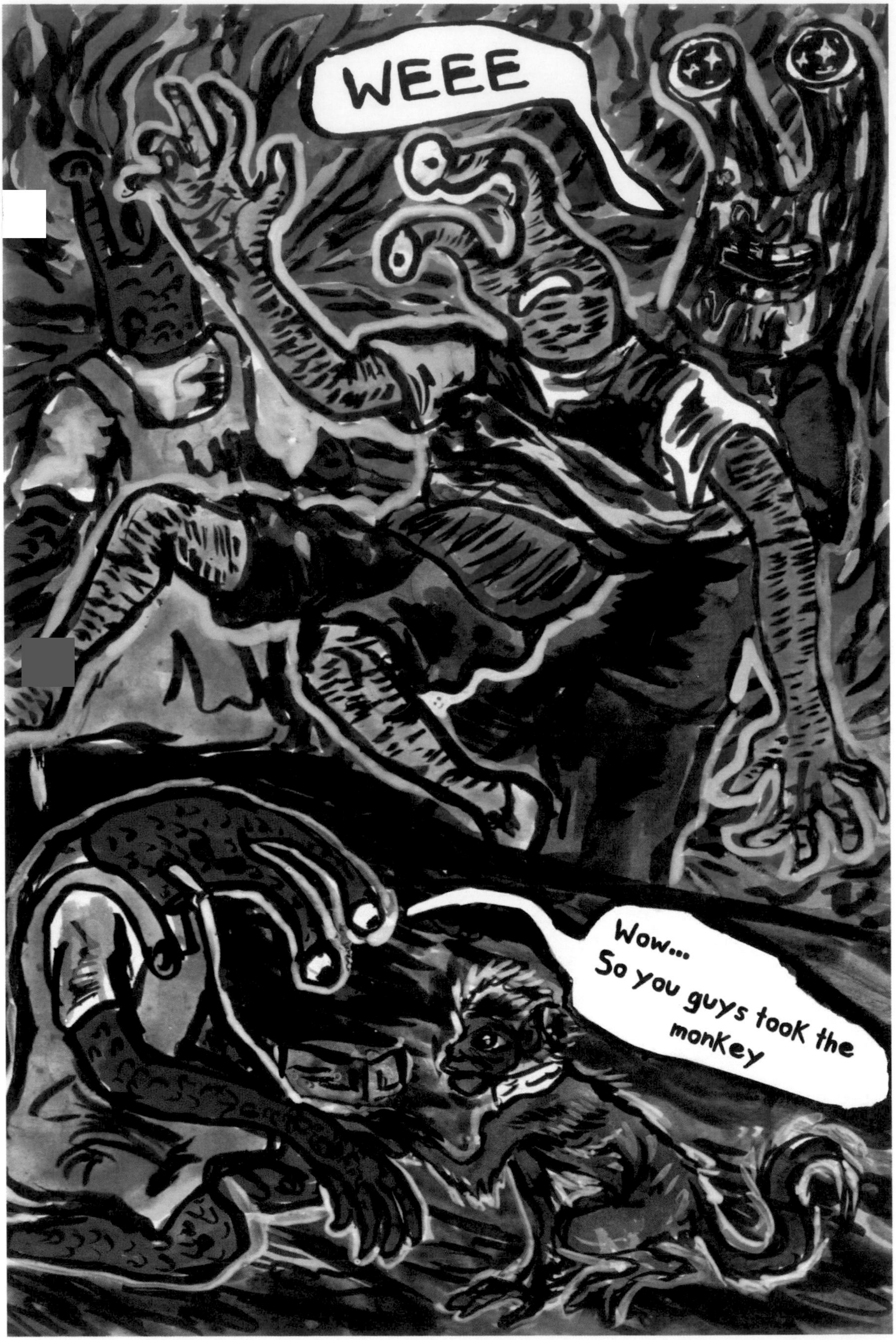
WEEE
Wow...
So you guys took the monkey

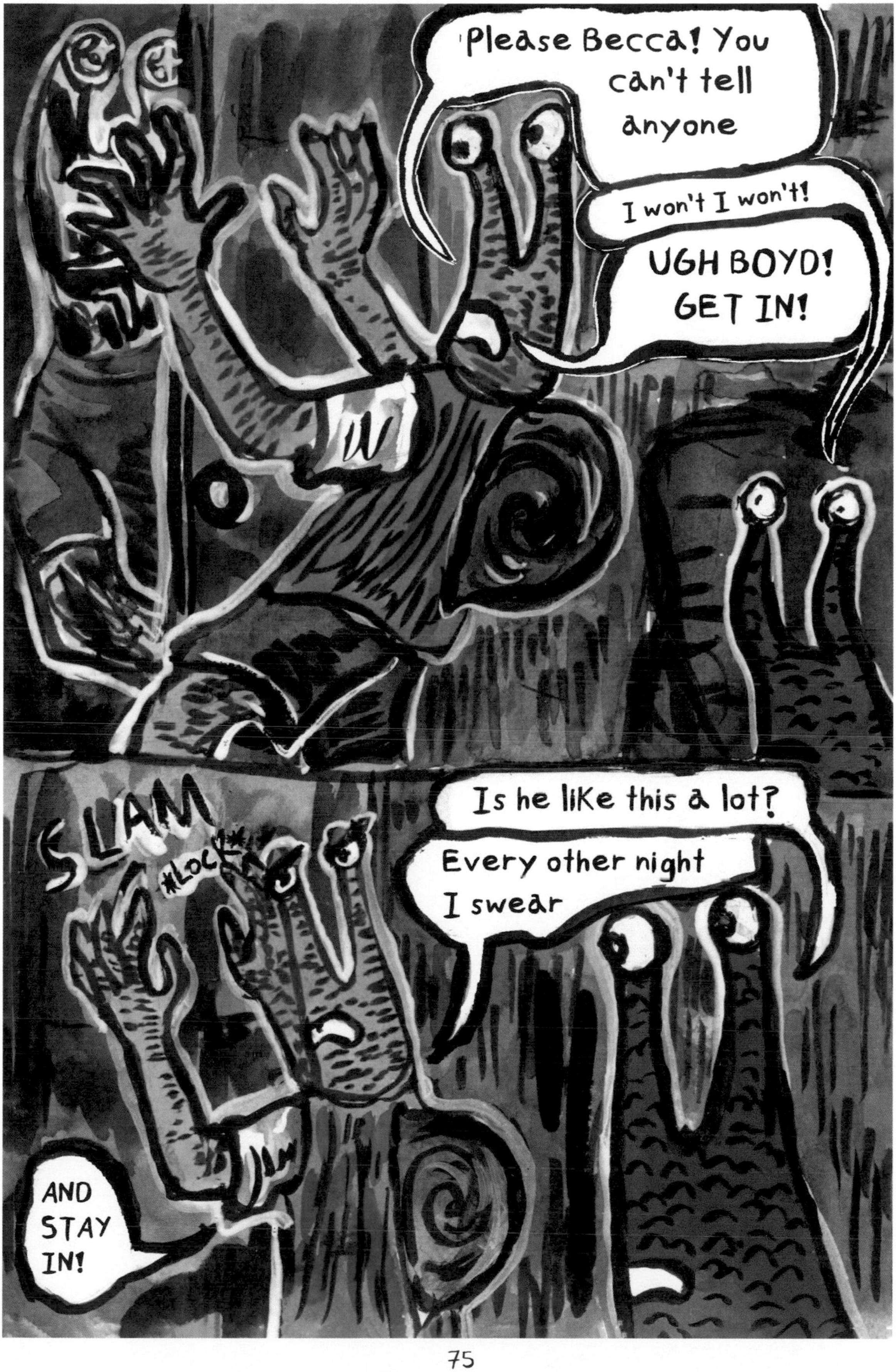
Please Becca! You can't tell anyone
I won't I won't!
UGH BOYD! GET IN!
SLAM
LOCK
Is he like this a lot?
Every other night I swear
AND STAY IN!

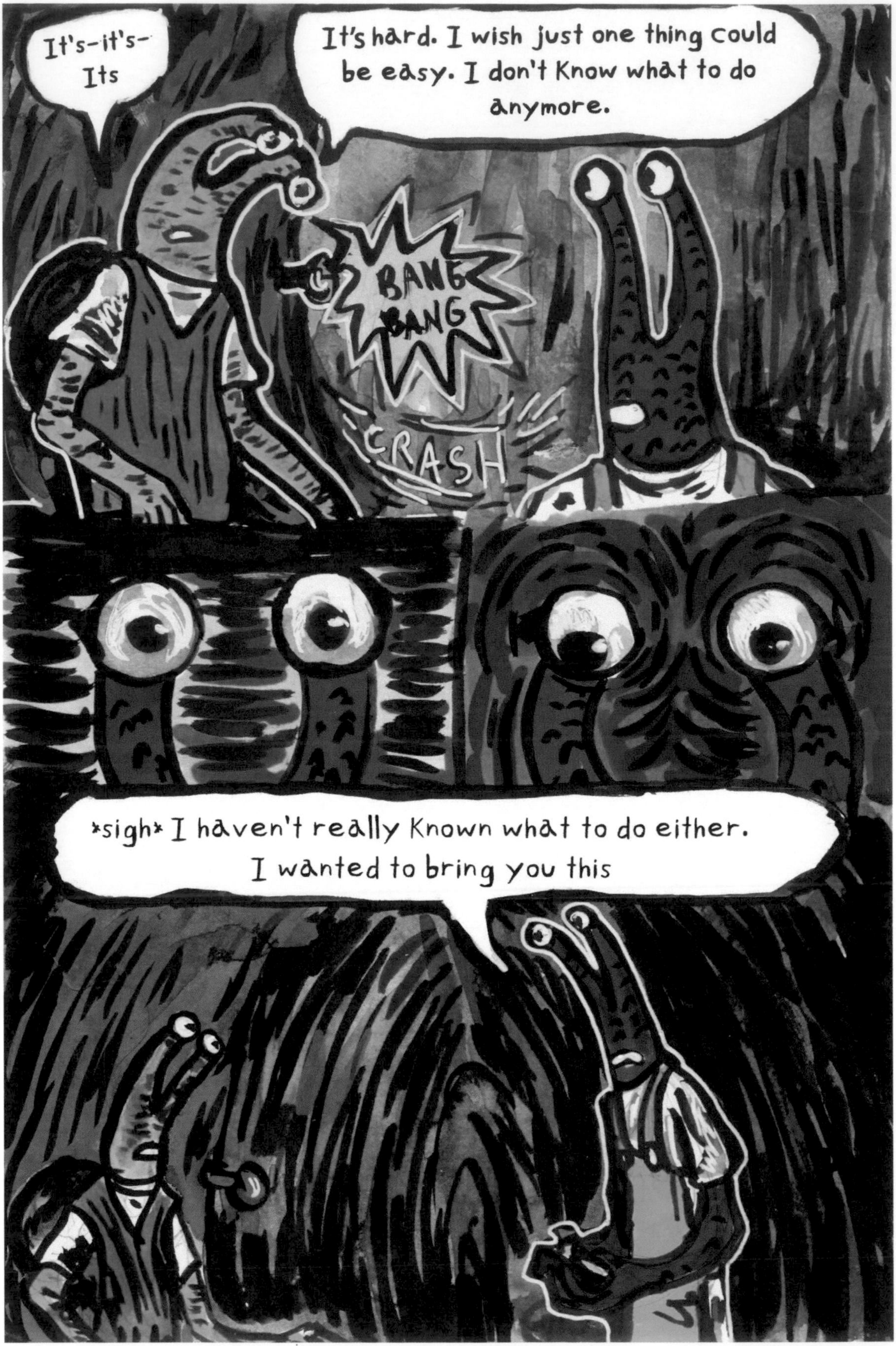
It's-it's-
Its
It's hard. I wish just one thing could be easy. I don't Know what to do anymore.
BANG BANG
CRASH
sigh I haven't really Known what to do either.
I wanted to bring you this

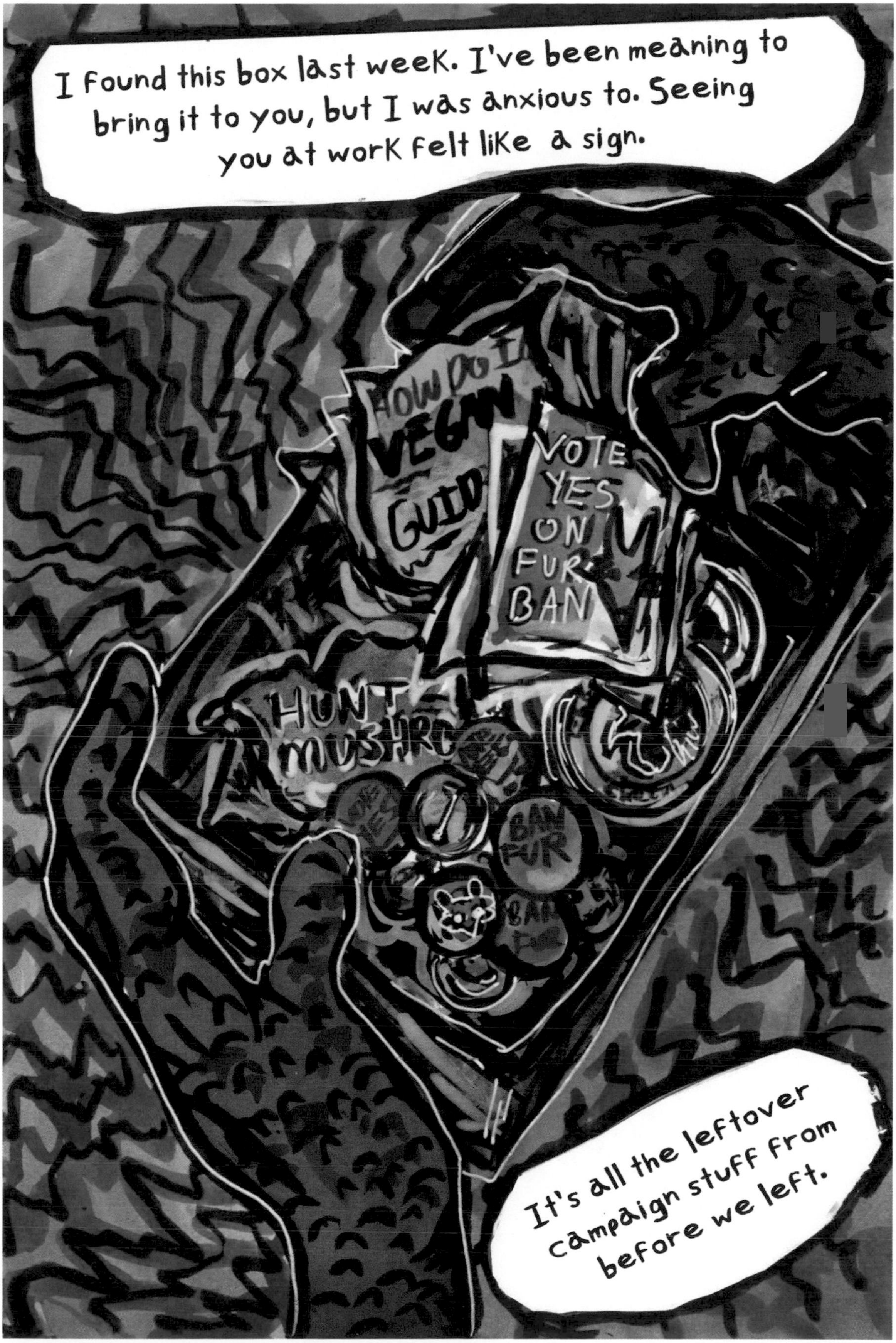
I found this box last week. I've been meaning to bring it to you, but I was anxious to. Seeing you at work felt like a sign.
VOTE YES ON FUR BAN
BAN FUR
It's all the leftover campaign stuff from before we left.

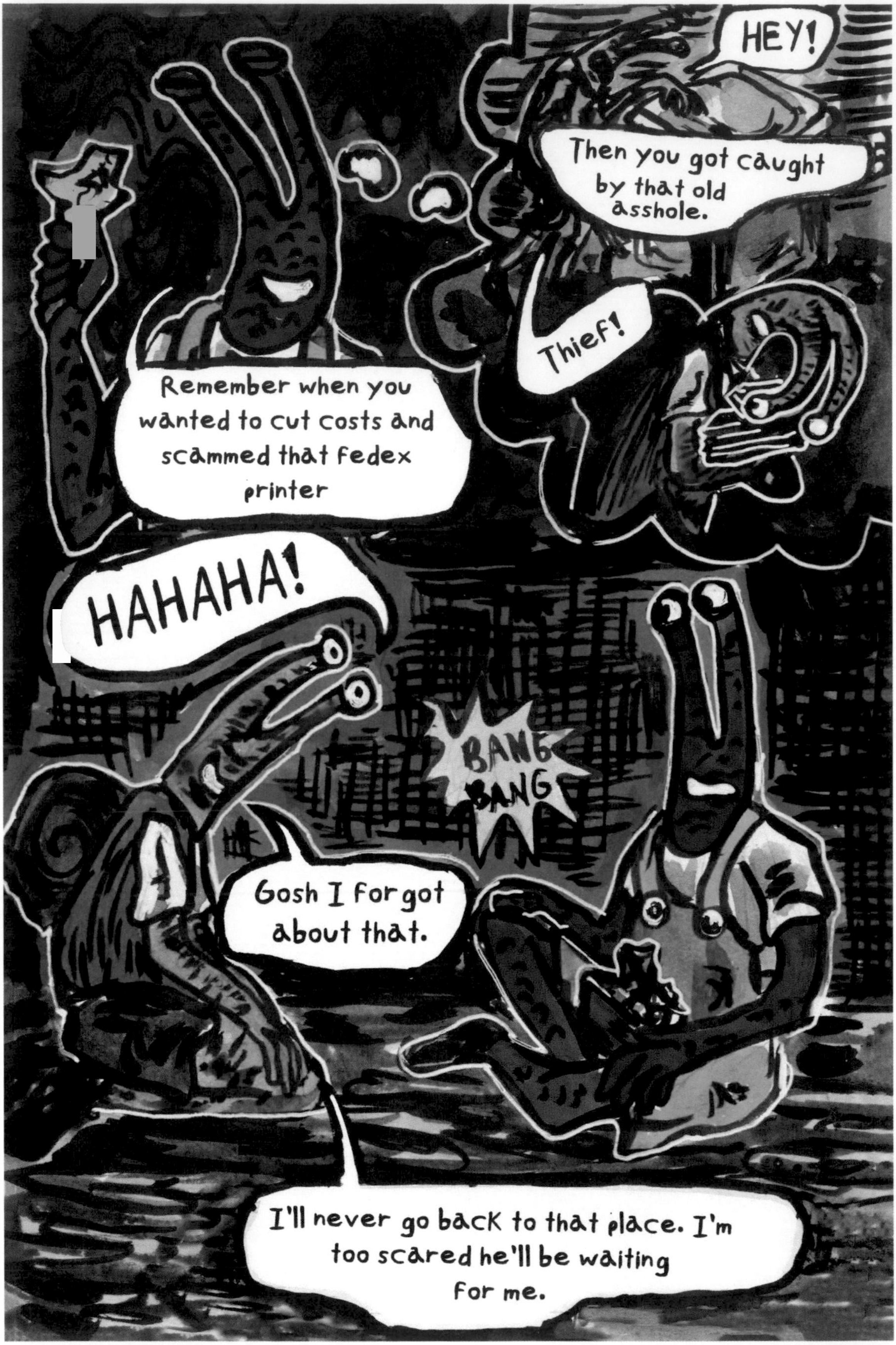
Remember when you wanted to cut costs and scammed that fedex printer
HEY!
Then you got caught by that old asshole.
Thief!
HAHAHA!
BANG BANG
Gosh I forgot about that.
I'll never go back to that place. I'm too scared he'll be waiting for me.

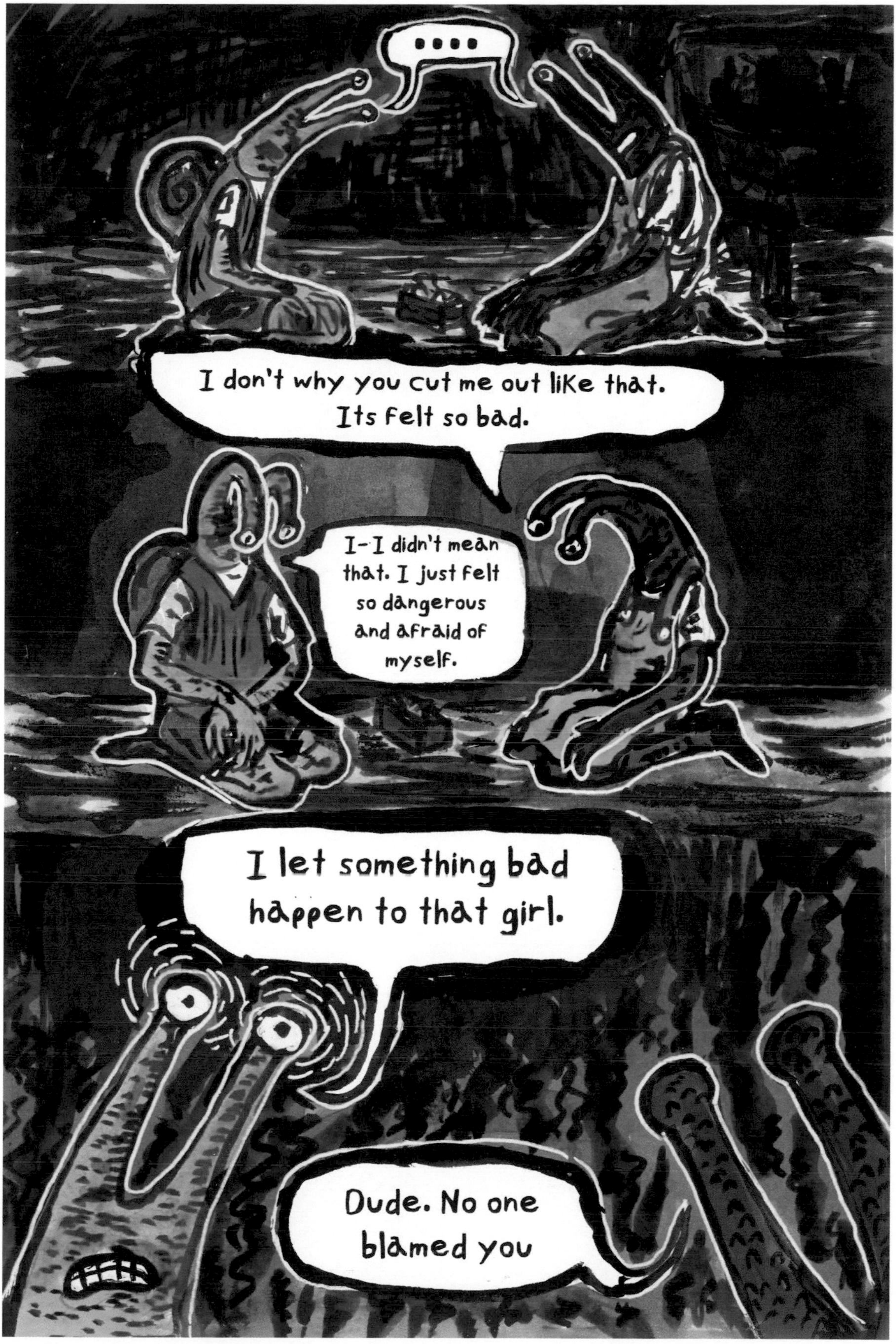
....
I don't why you cut me out like that. Its felt so bad.
I-I didn't mean that. I just felt so dangerous and afraid of myself.
I let something bad happen to that girl.
Dude. No one blamed you

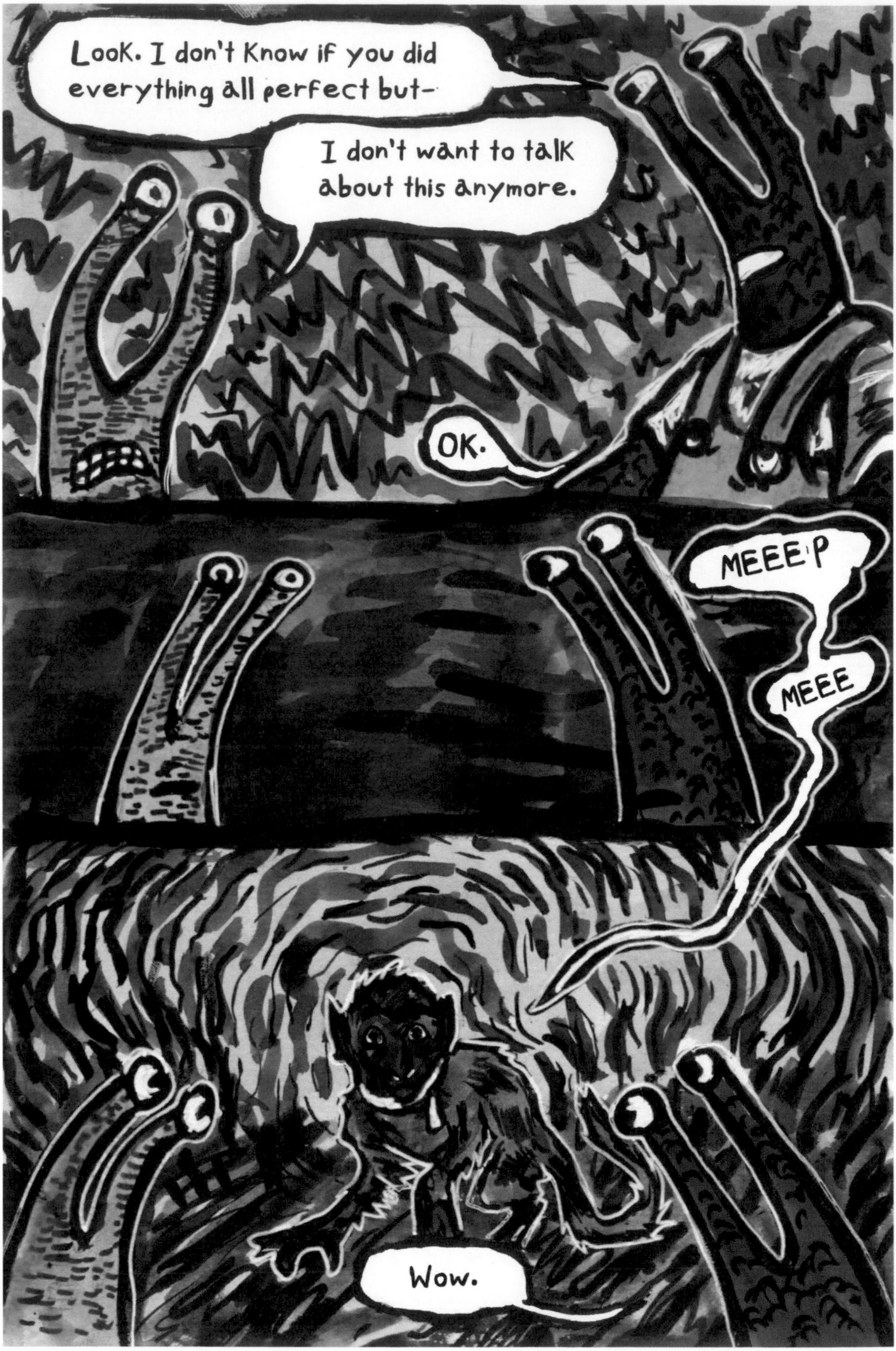
Look. I don't Know if you did everything all perfect but-
I don't want to talk about this anymore.
OK.
MEEEP
MEEE
Wow.

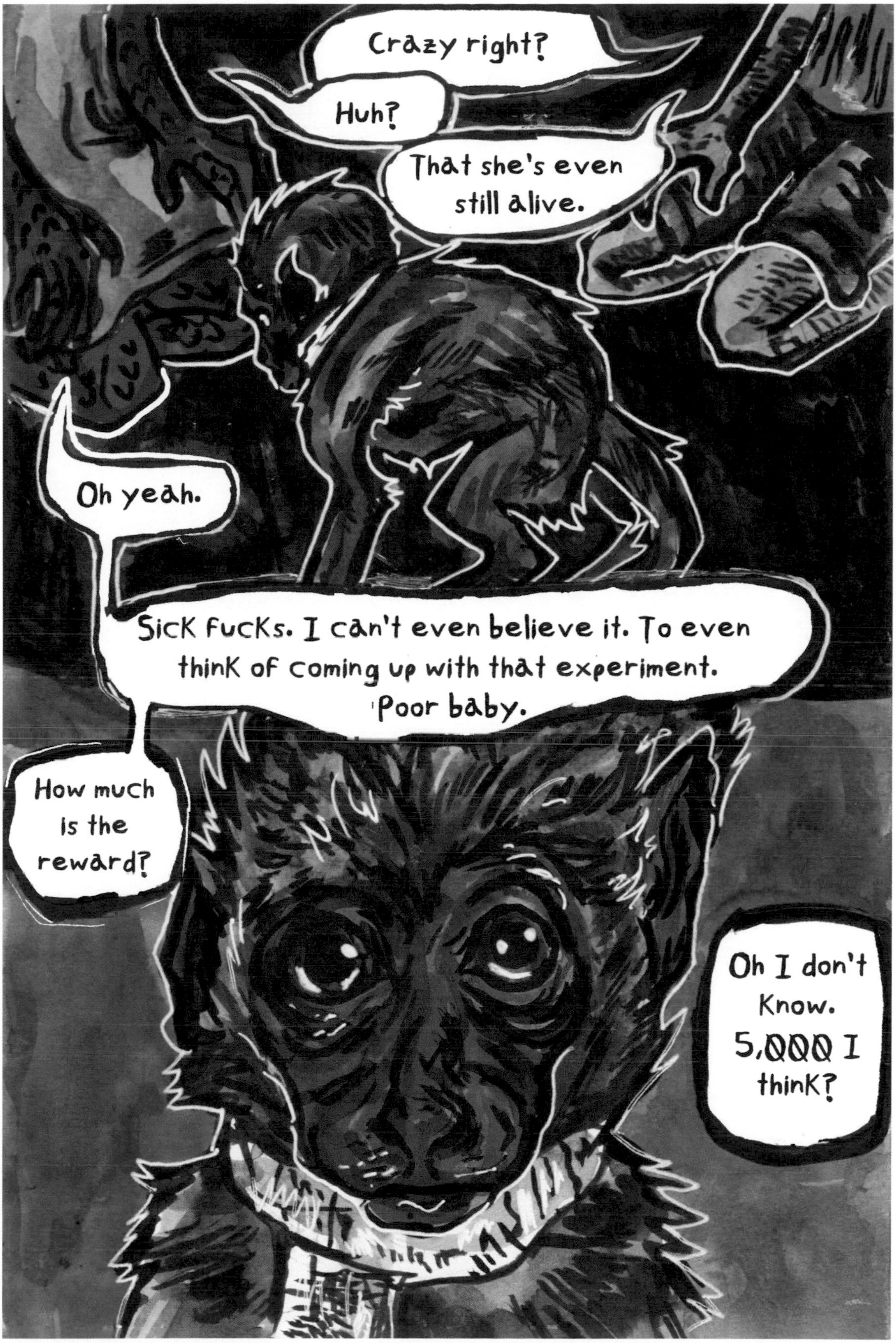
Crazy right?
Huh?
That she's even still alive.
Oh yeah.
Sick fucks. I can't even believe it. To even think of coming up with that experiment. Poor baby.
How much is the reward?
Oh I don't know. 5,000 I think?

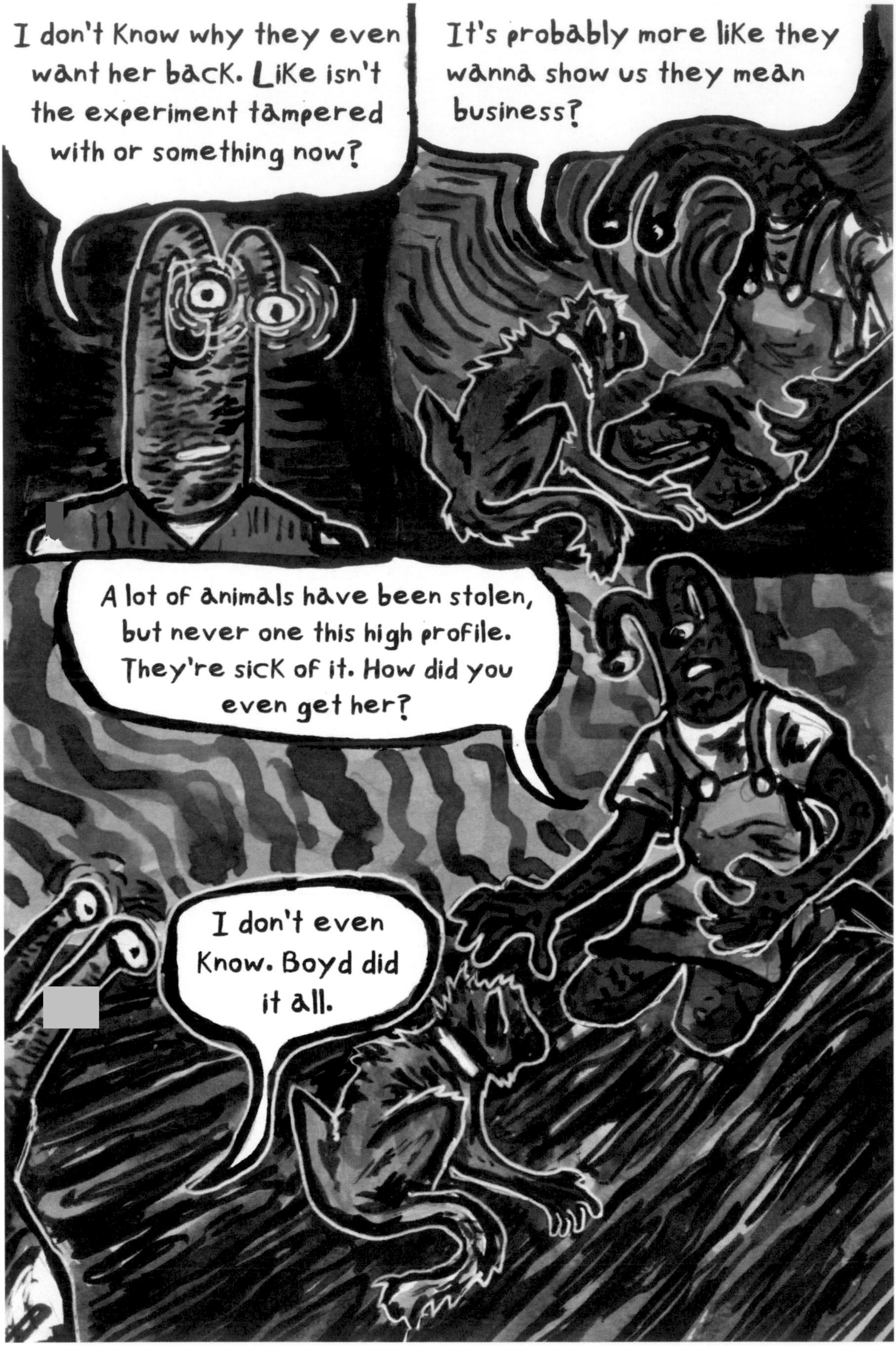
I don't Know why they even want her back. Like isn't the experiment tampered with or something now?
It's probably more like they wanna show us they mean business?
A lot of animals have been stolen, but never one this high profile. They're sick of it. How did you even get her?
I don't even Know. Boyd did it all.

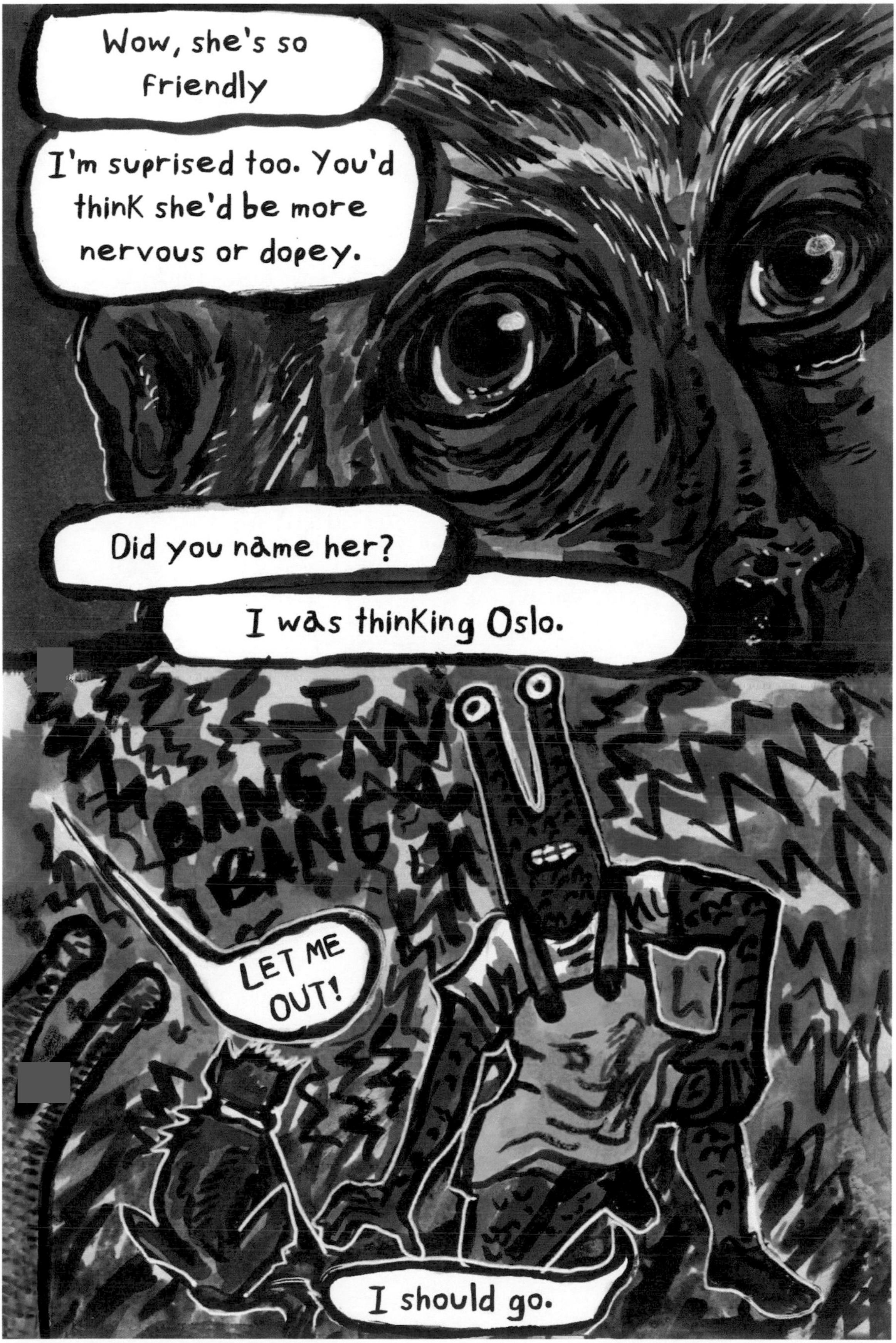
Wow, she's so friendly
I'm suprised too. You'd think she'd be more nervous or dopey.
Did you name her?
I was thinking Oslo.
BANG
BANG
LET ME OUT!
I should go.

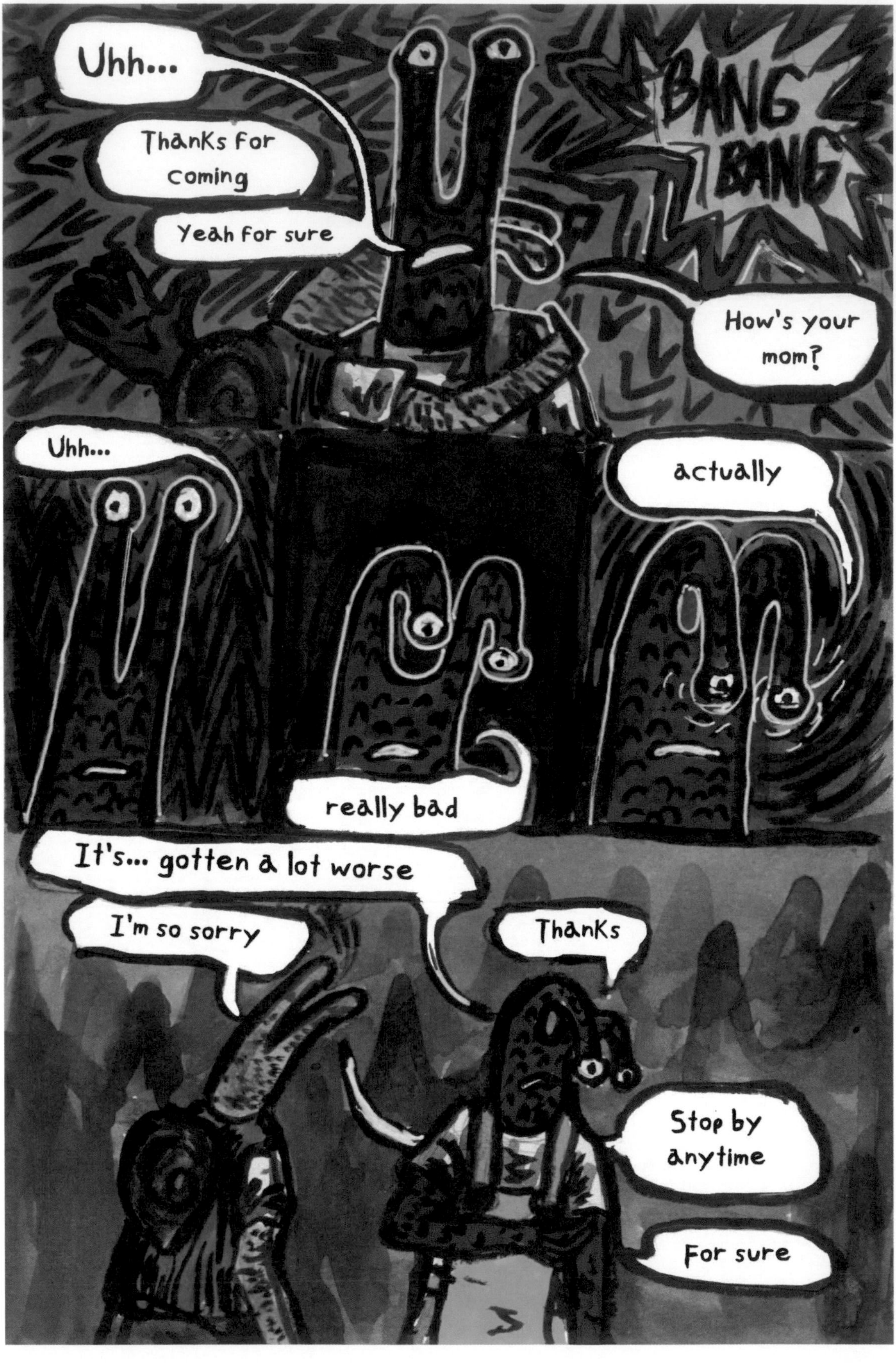
Uhh...
Thanks for coming
Yeah for sure
BANG BANG
How's your mom?
Uhh...
actually
really bad
It's... gotten a lot worse
I'm so sorry
Thanks
Stop by anytime
For sure

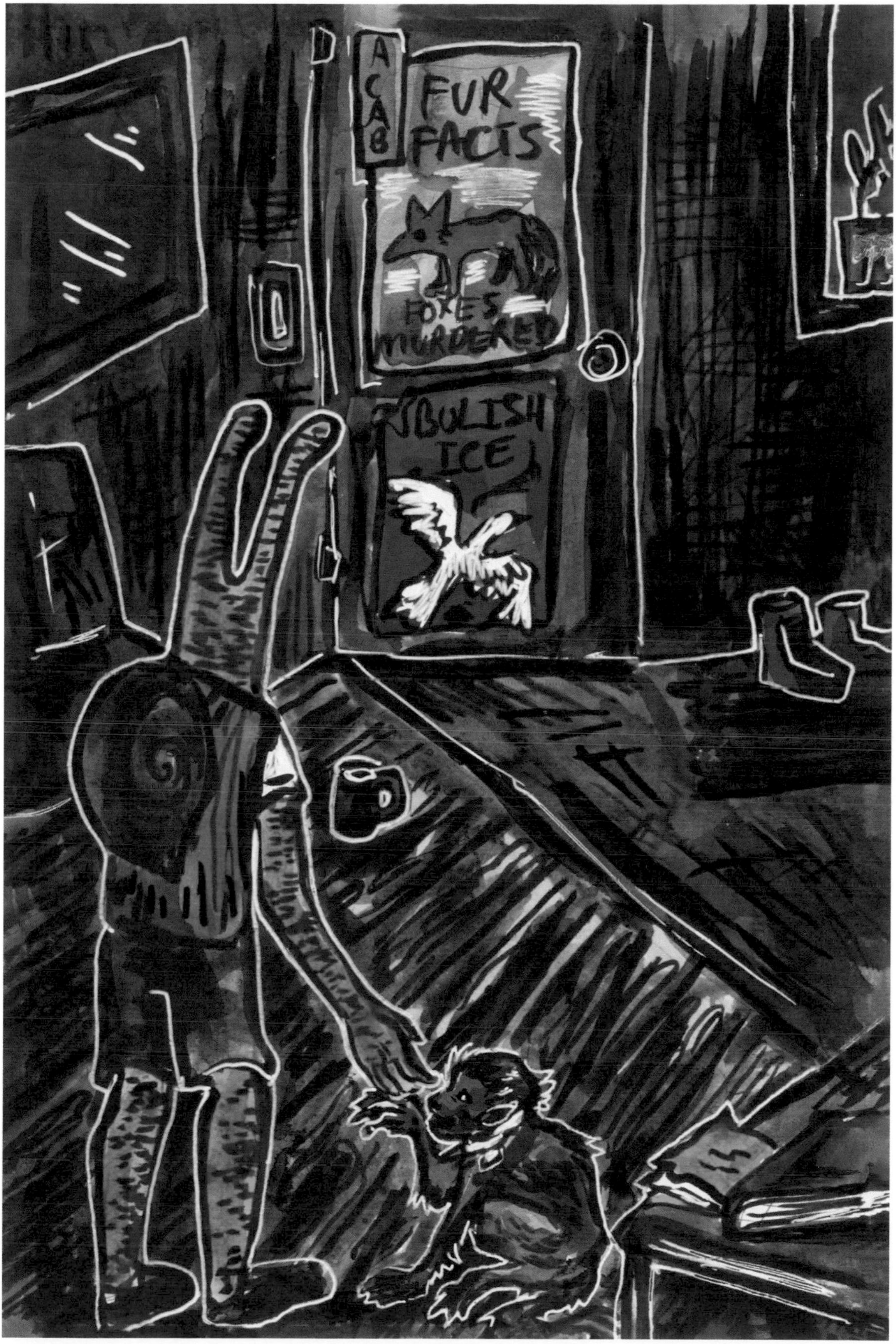
ACAB
FUR FACTS
FOXES MURDERED
ABOLISH ICE

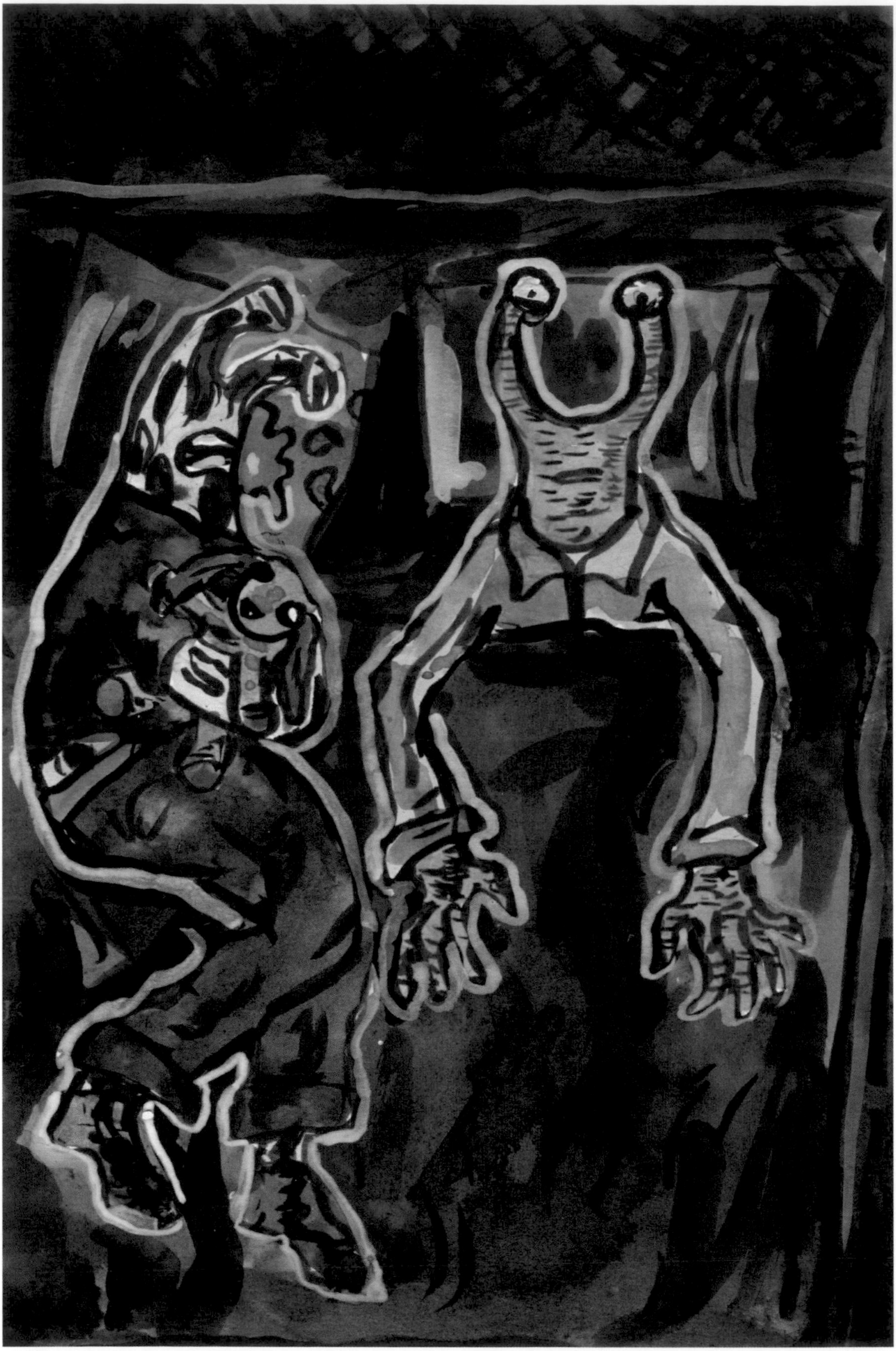

CHAPTER 5

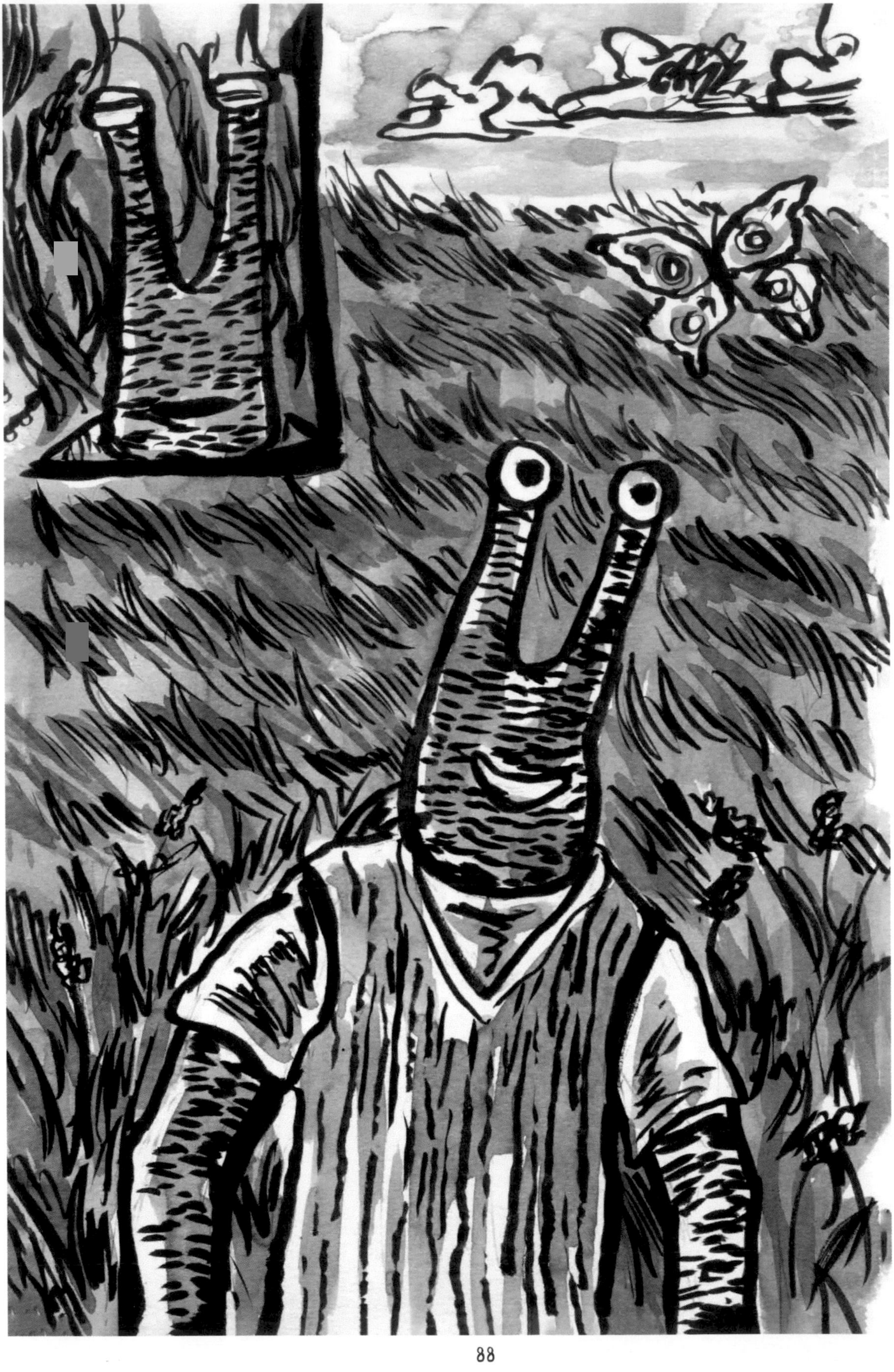

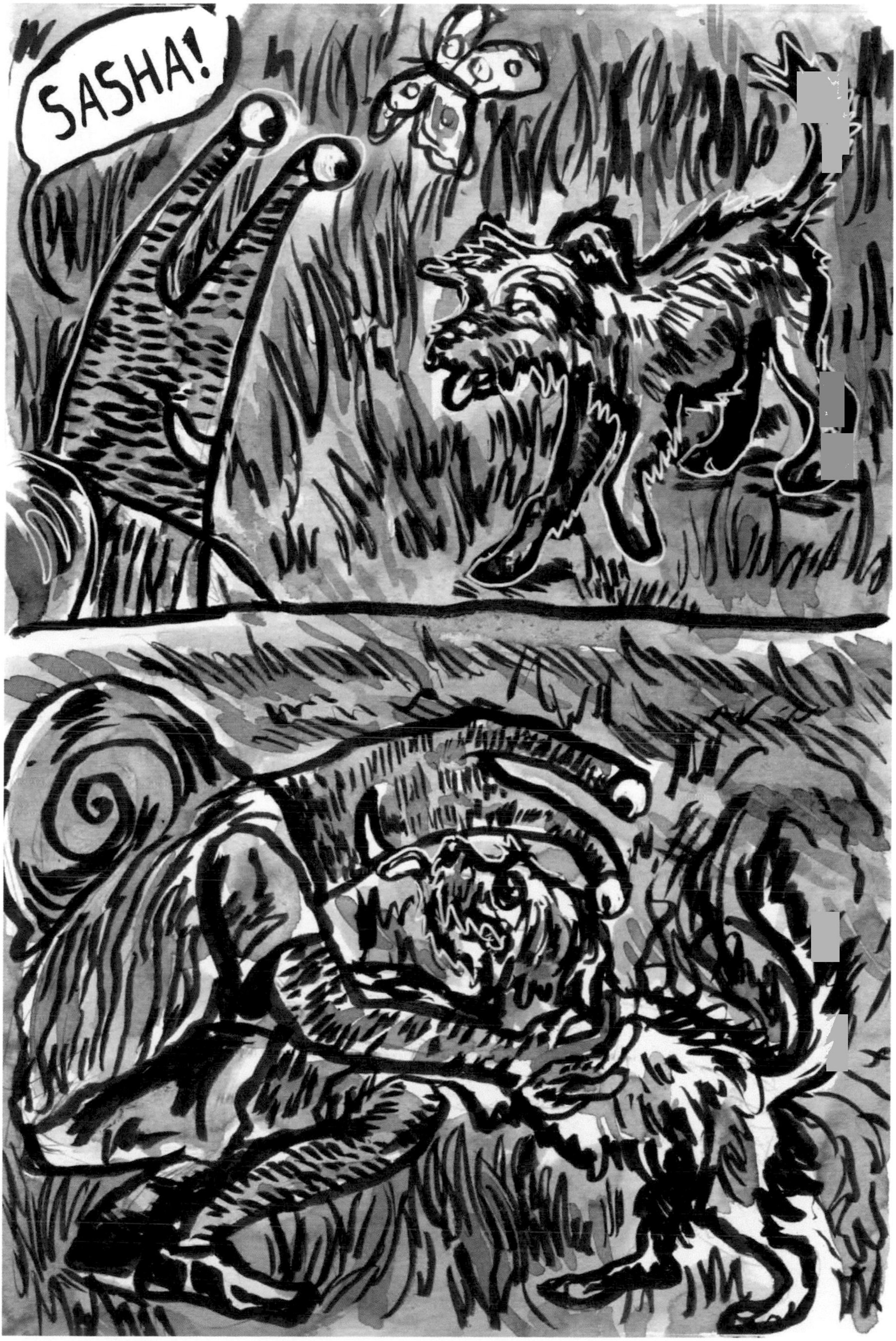
SASHA!

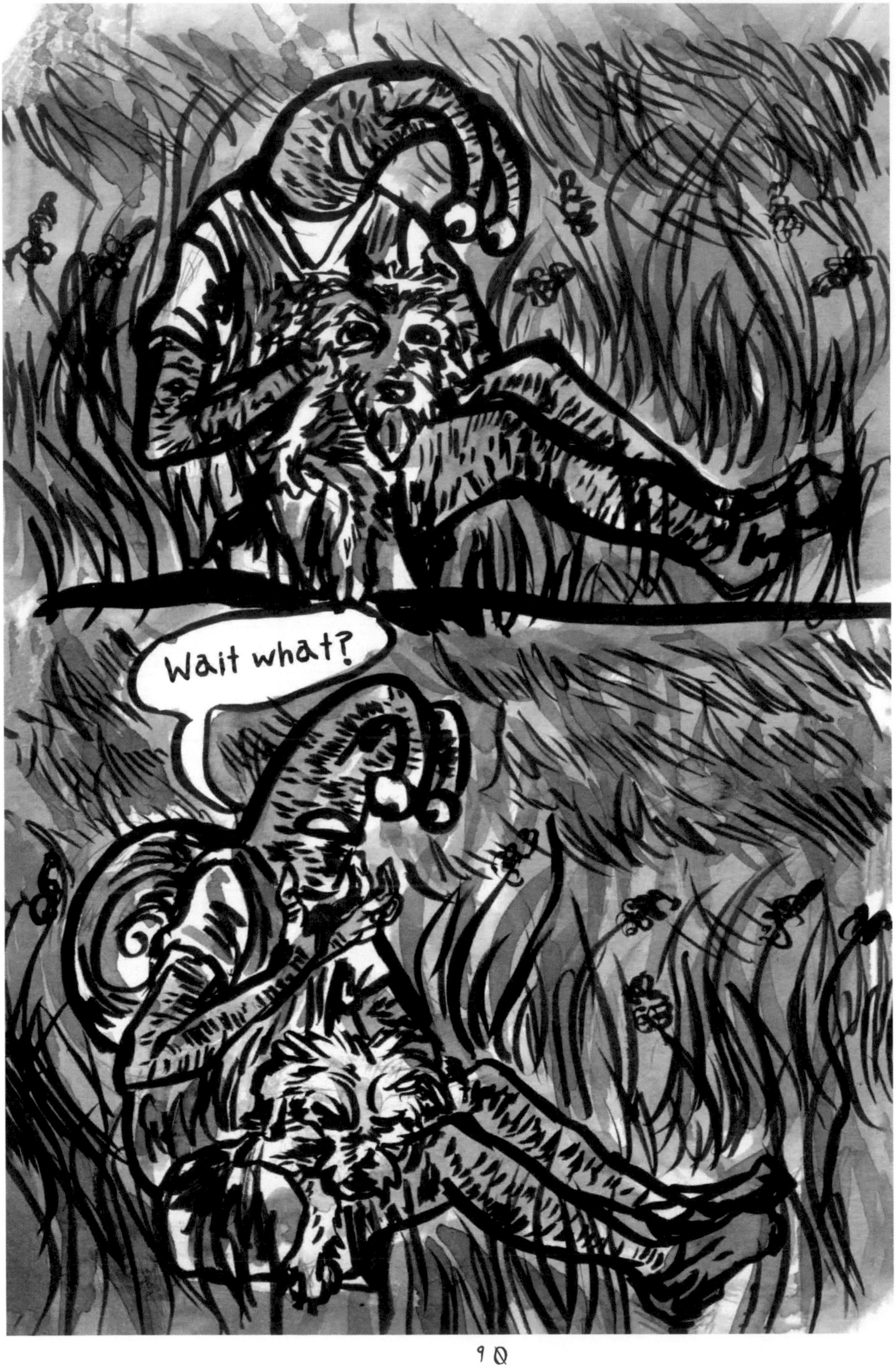
Wait what?

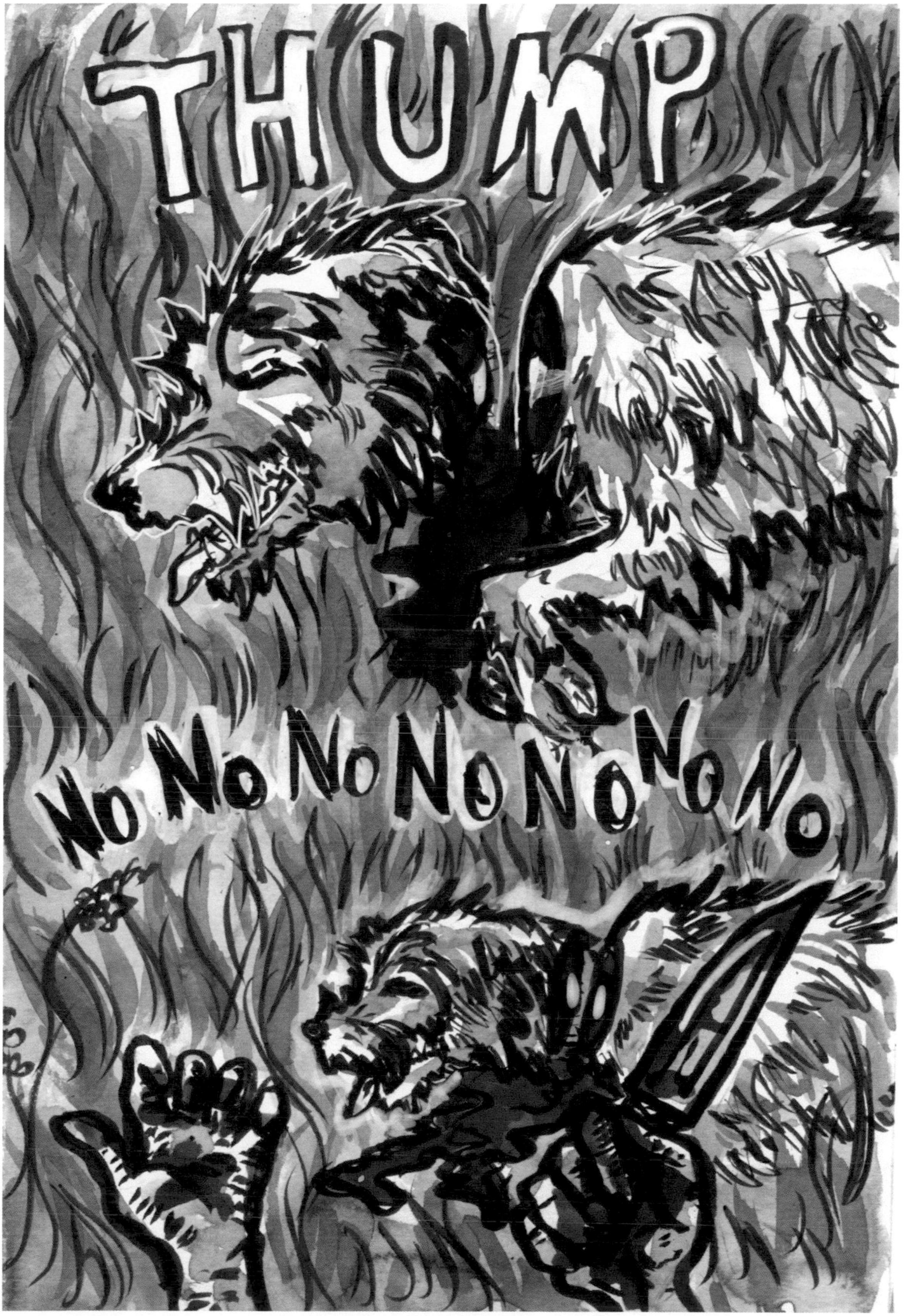
THUMP
NO NO NO NO NO NO NO

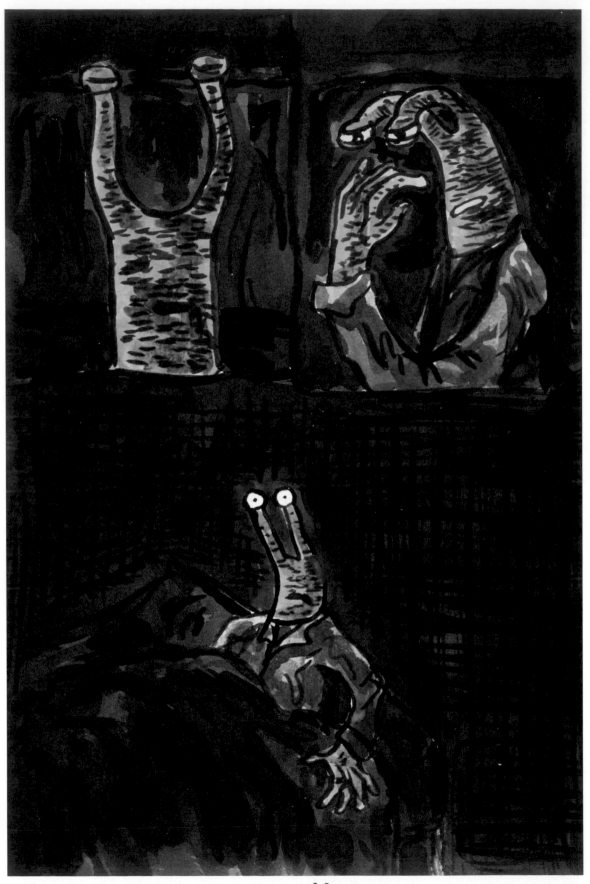

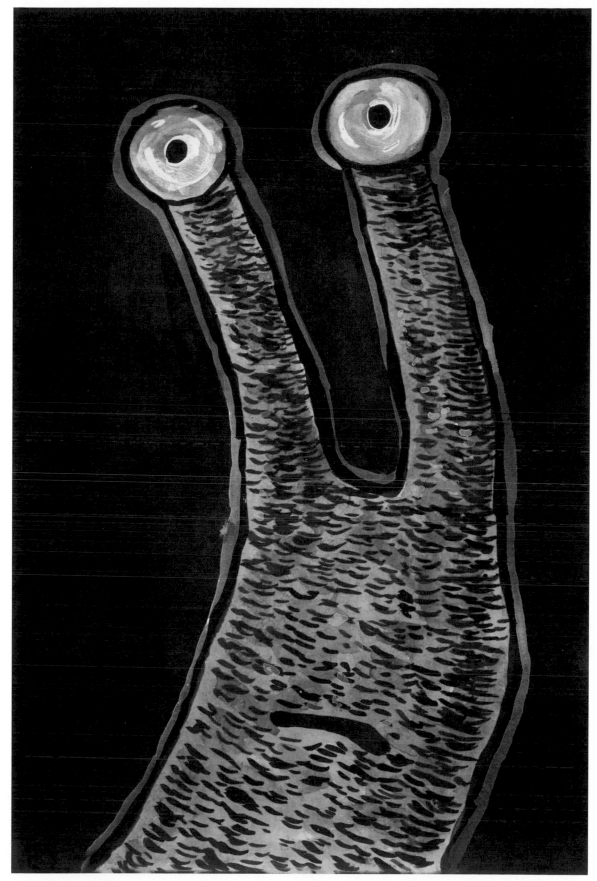

93

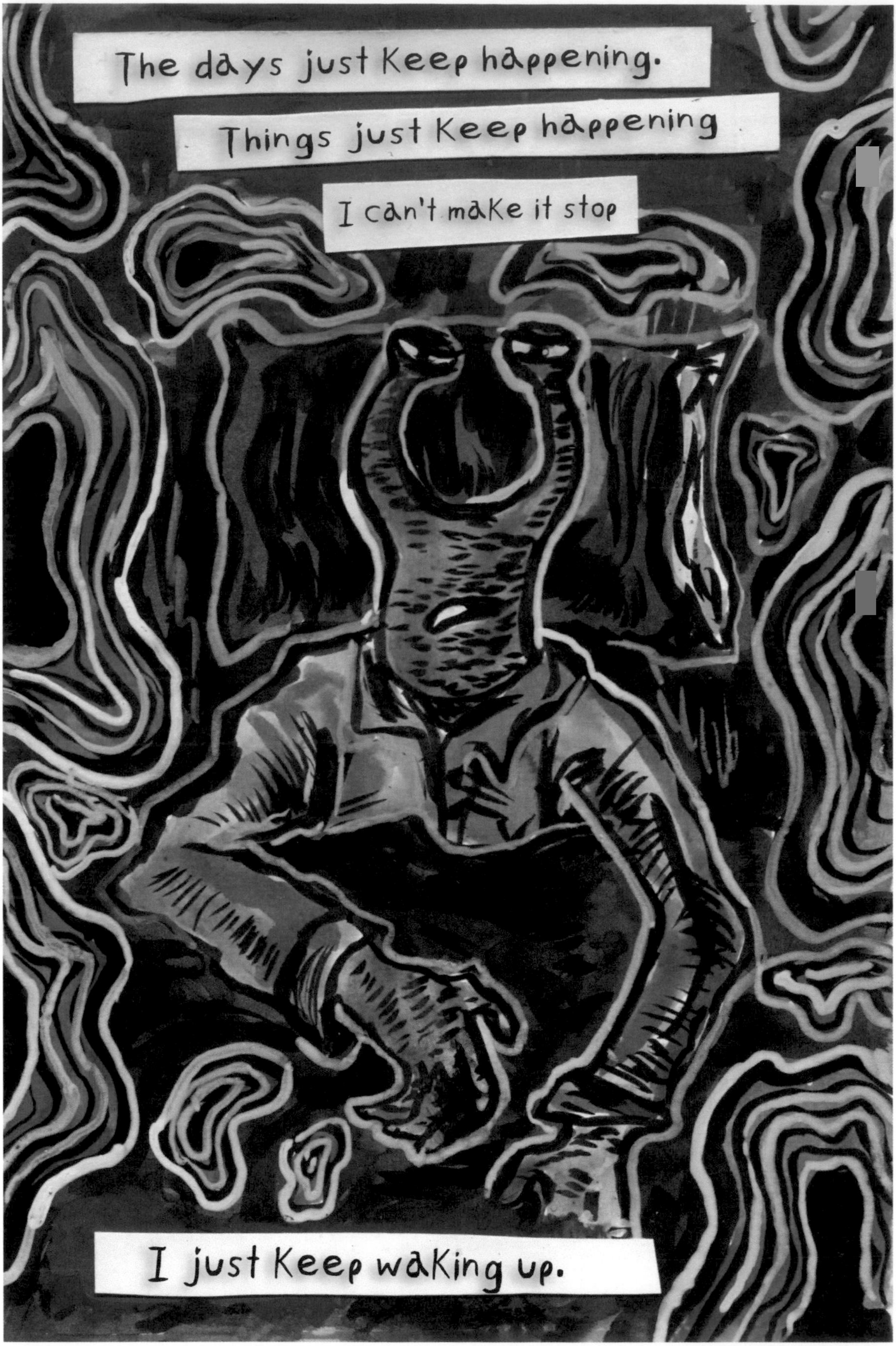
The days just Keep happening.
Things just Keep happening
I can't make it stop
I just Keep waking up.

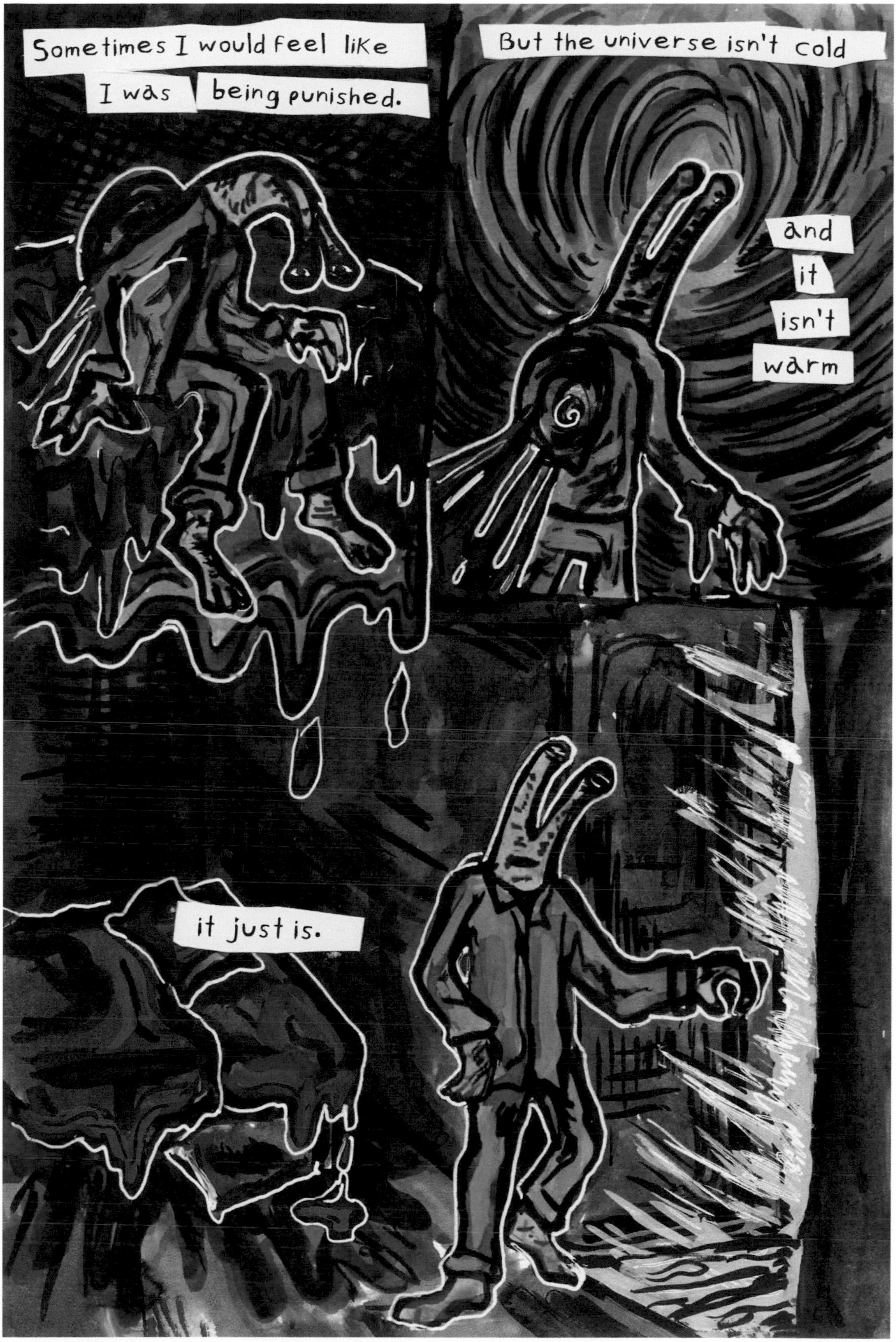
Sometimes I would feel like
I was being punished.
But the universe isn't cold
and it isn't warm
it just is.

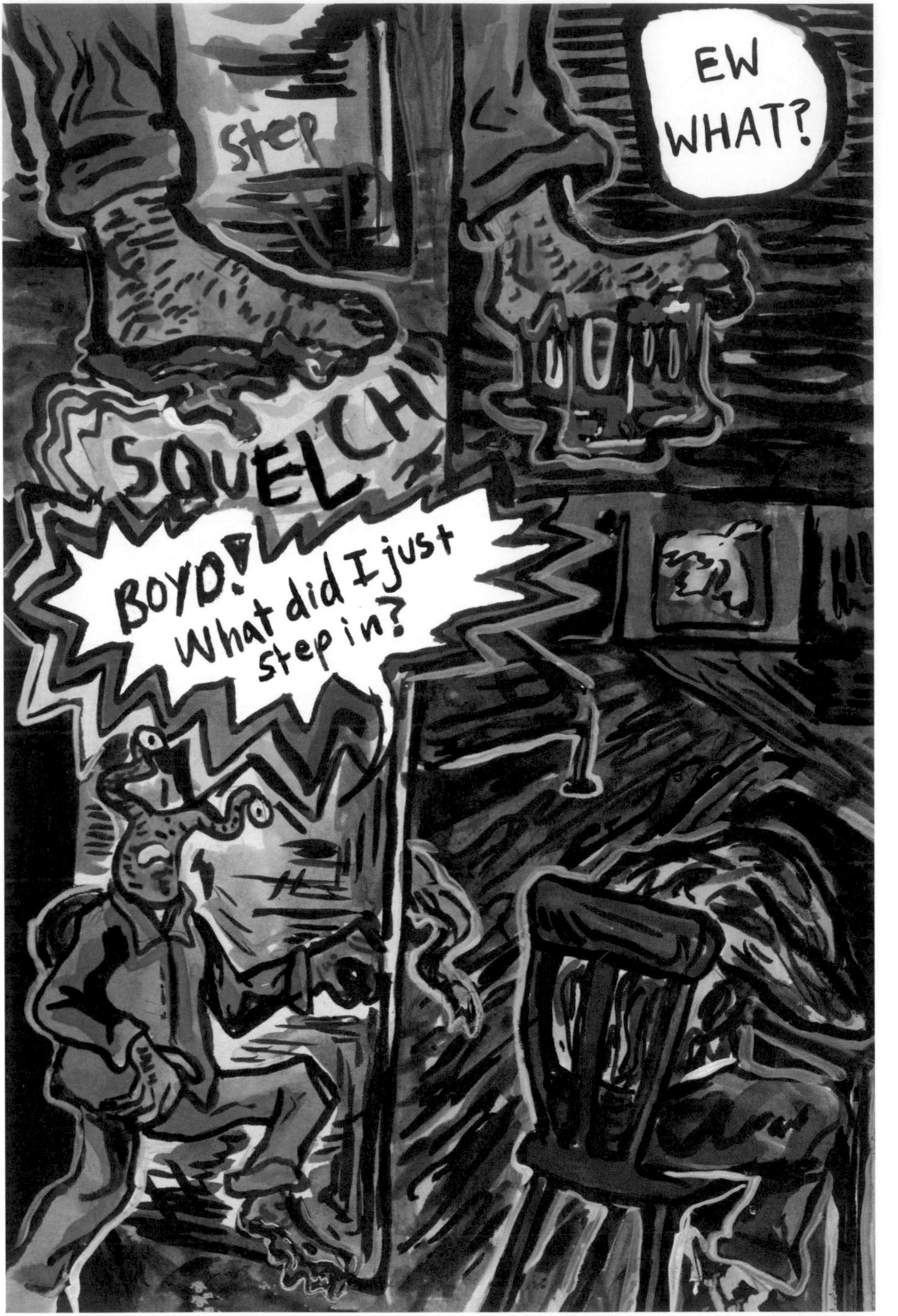
step
EW WHAT?
SQUELCH
BOYD! What did I just step in?

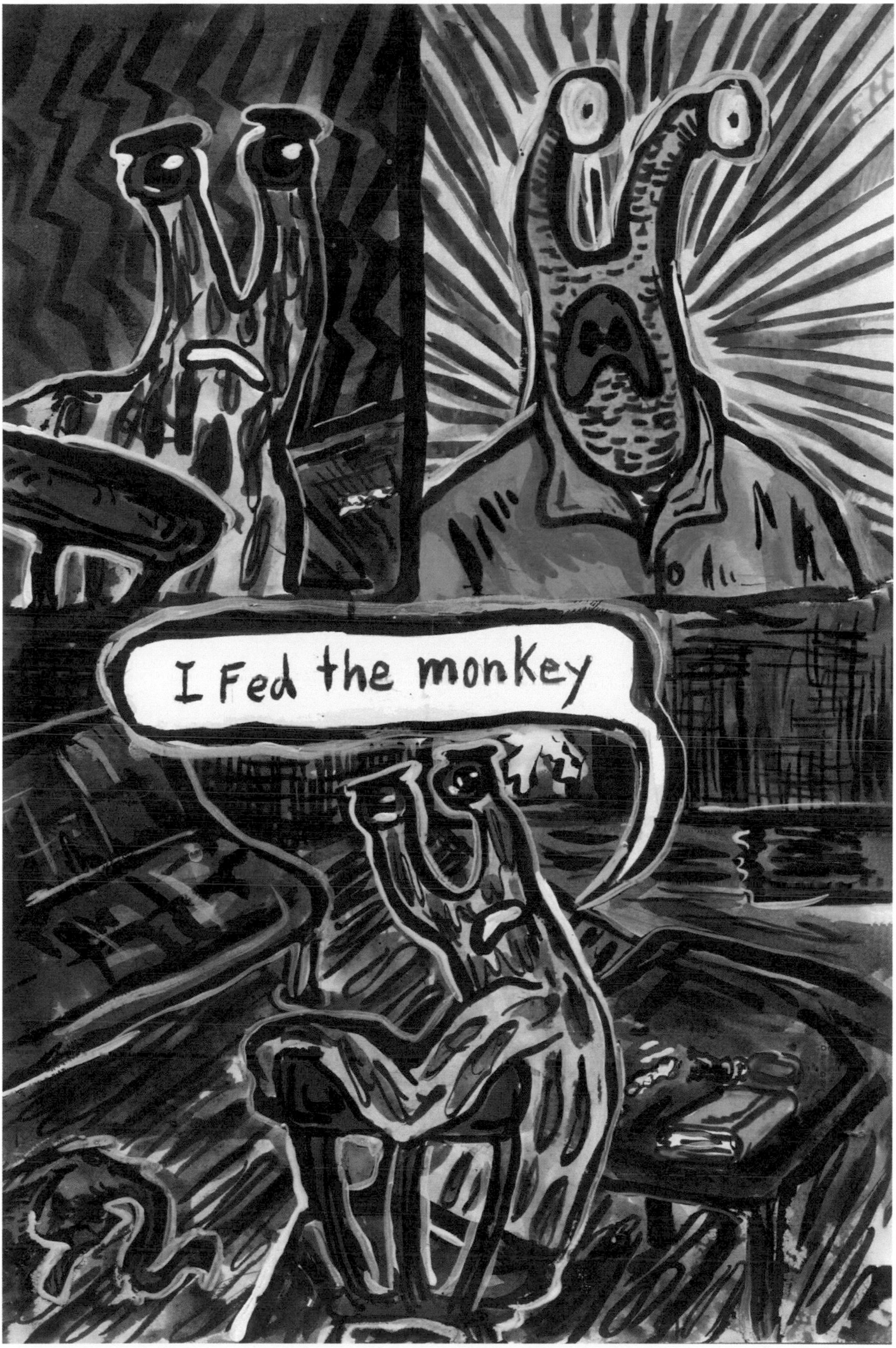
I Fed the monkey

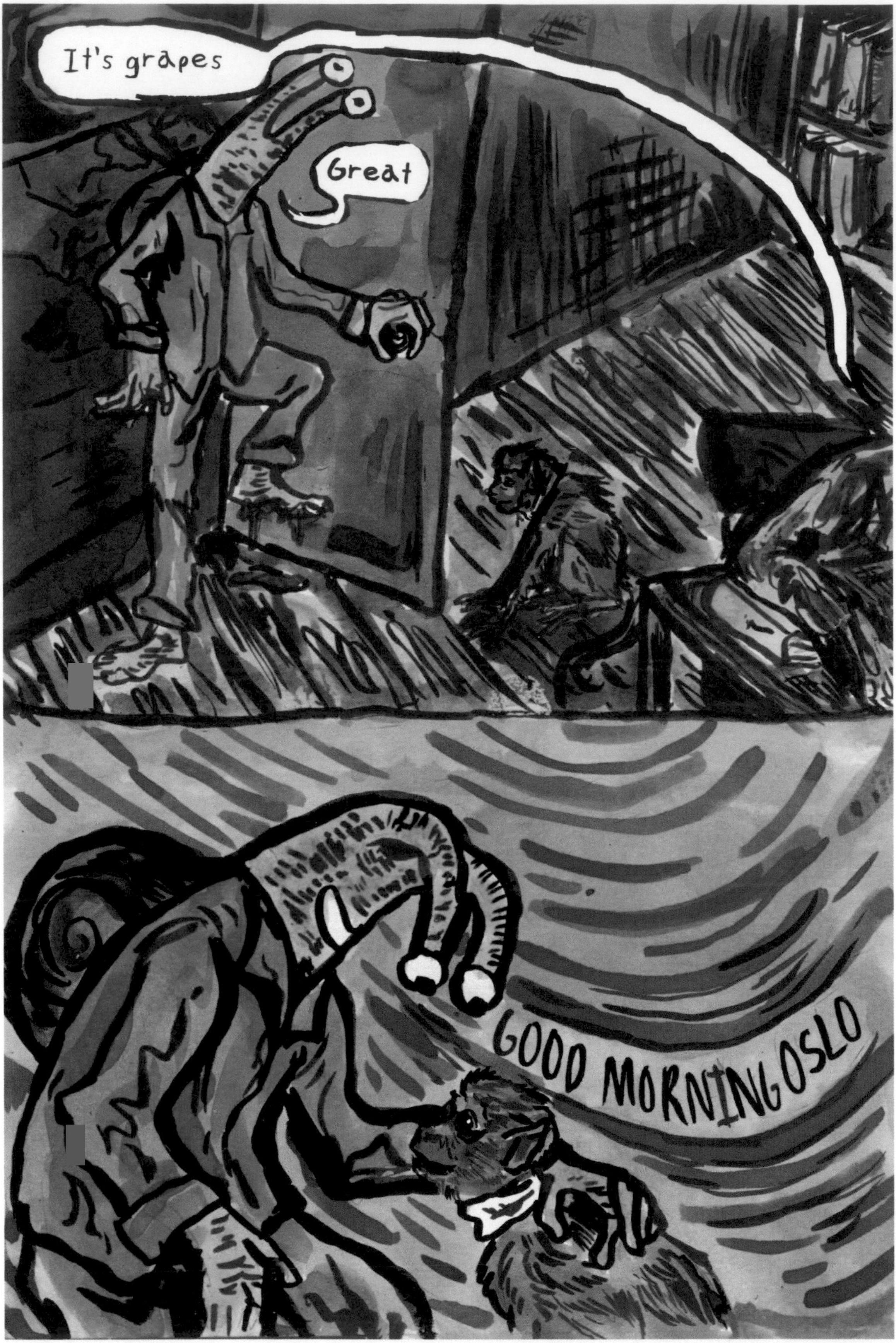
It's grapes
Great
GOOD MORNINGOSLO

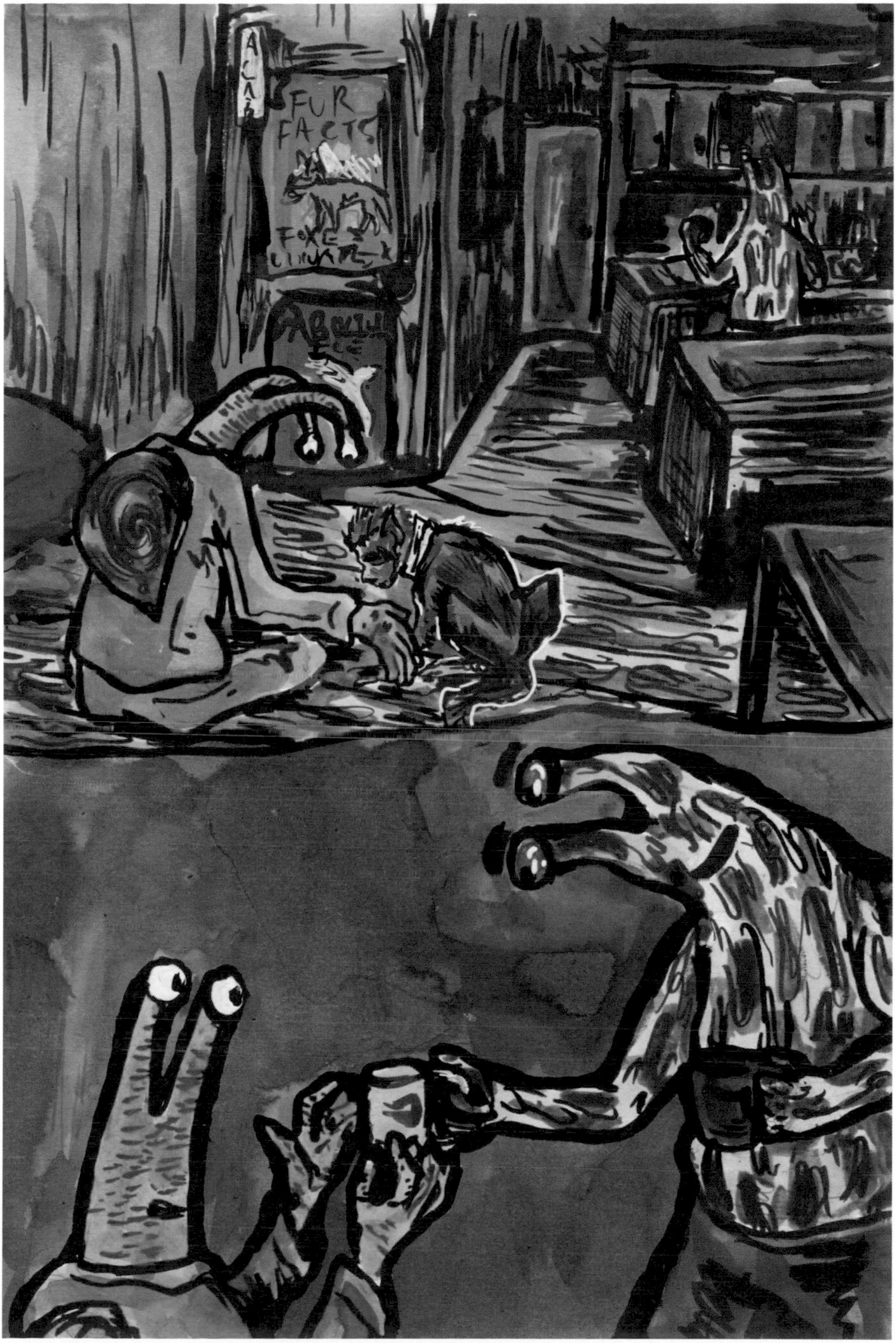
FUR FACTS

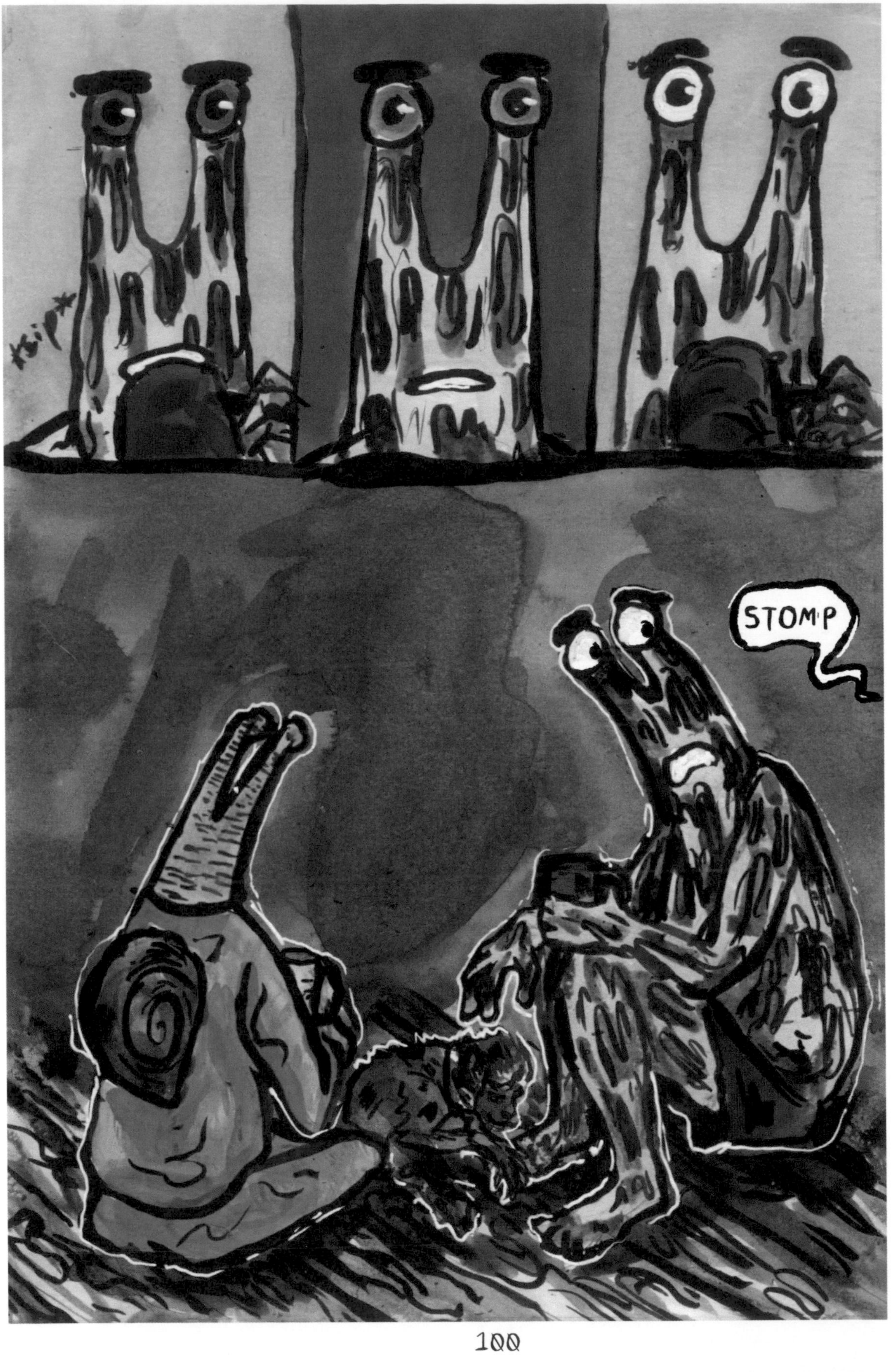
tsip
STOMP

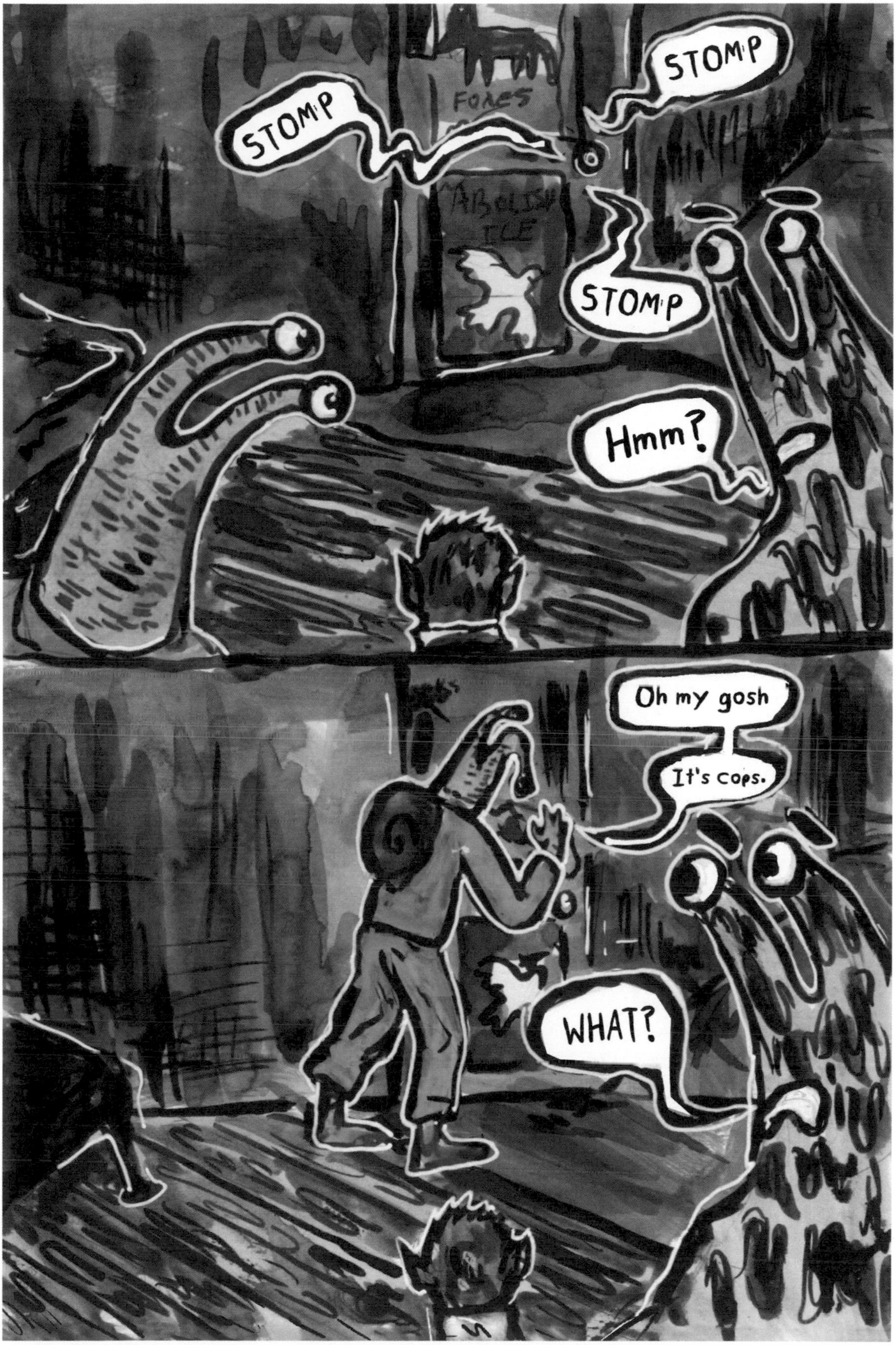
STOMP
STOMP
STOMP
FOXES
ABOLISH ICE
Hmm?
Oh my gosh
It's cops.
WHAT?

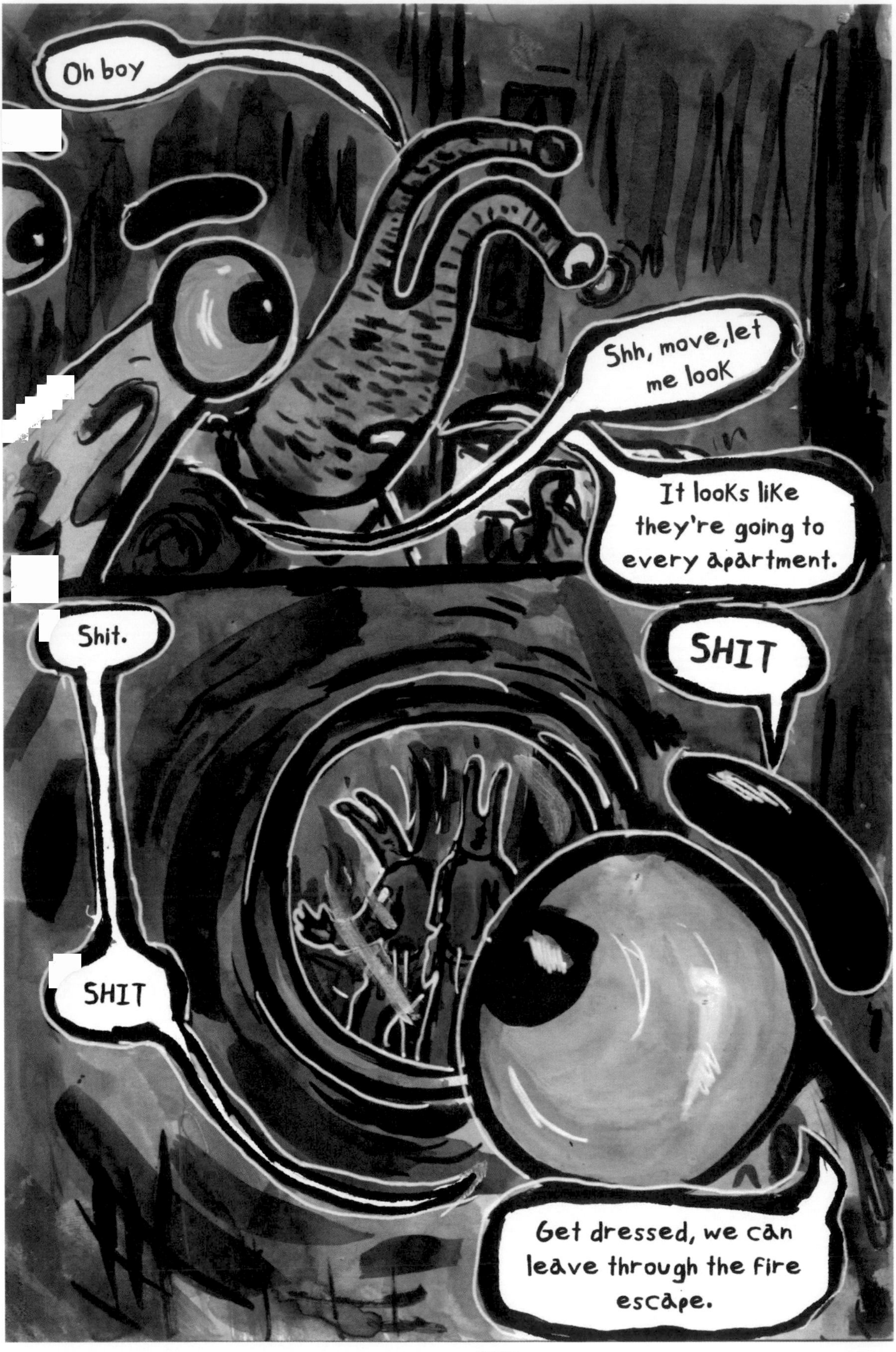
Oh boy
Shh, move, let me look
It looks like they're going to every apartment.
Shit.
SHIT
SHIT
Get dressed, we can leave through the fire escape.

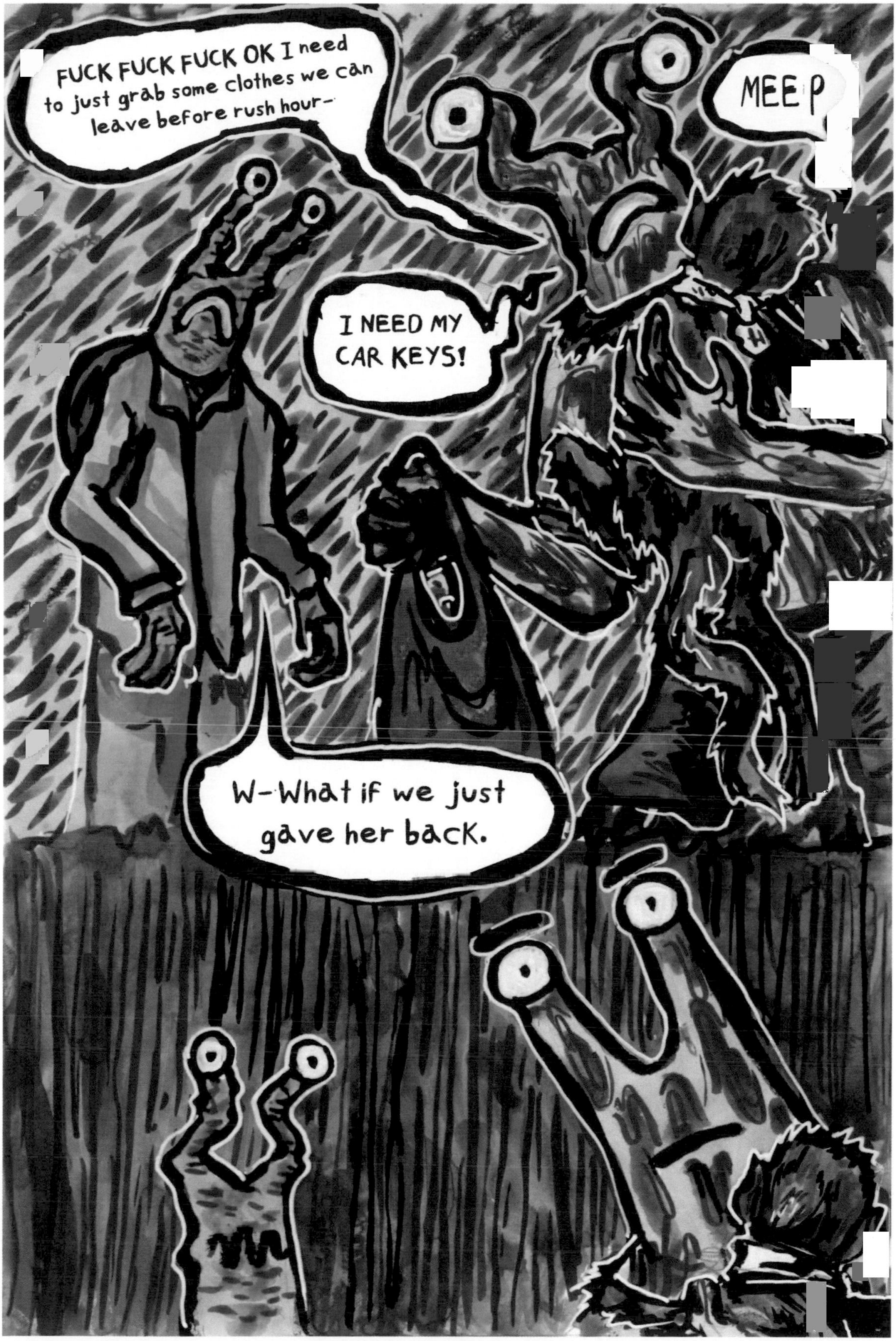
FUCK FUCK FUCK OK I need to just grab some clothes we can leave before rush hour-
MEEP
I NEED MY CAR KEYS!
W-What if we just gave her back.

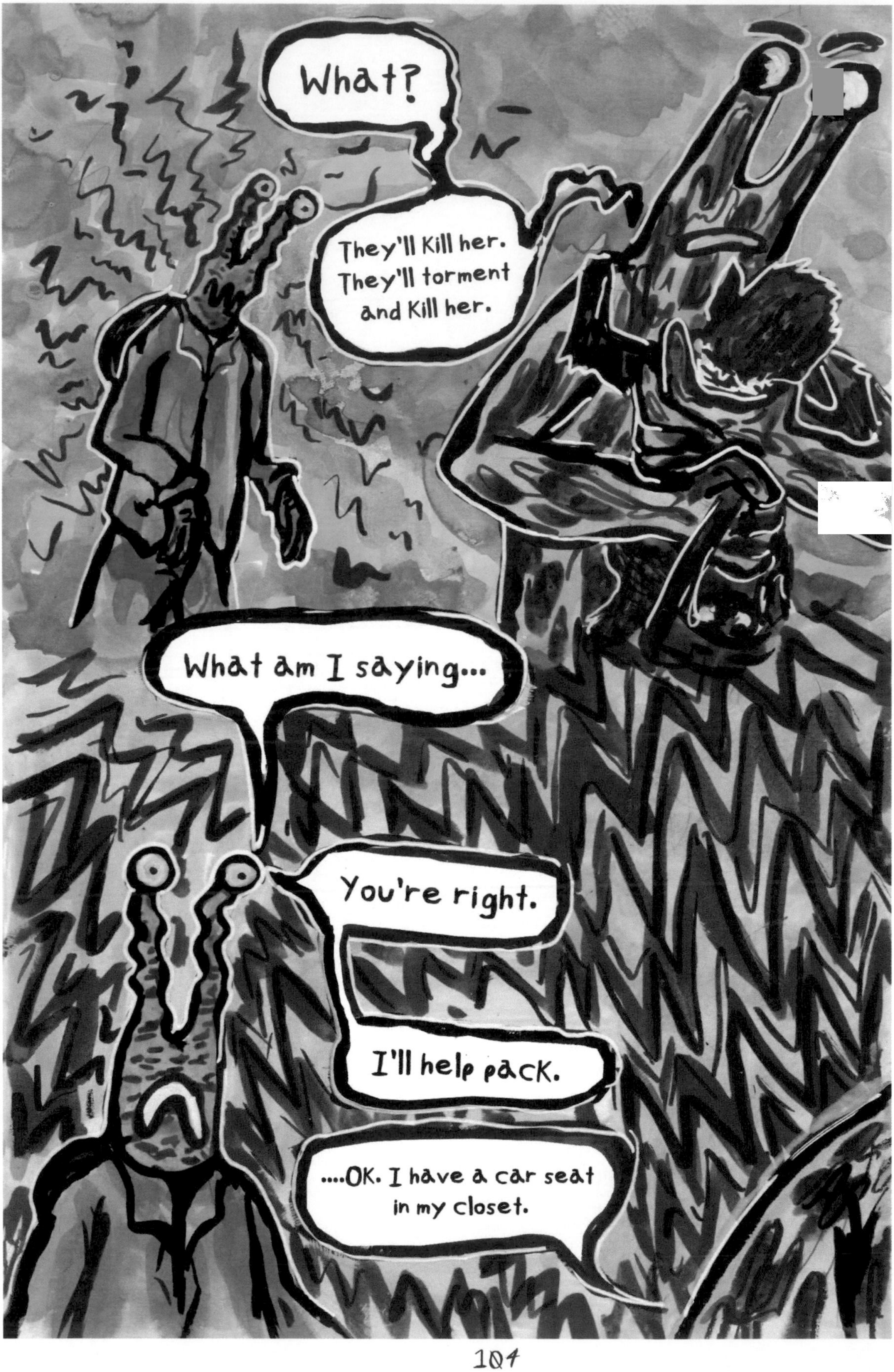
What?
They'll Kill her. They'll torment and Kill her.
What am I saying...
You're right.
I'll help pack.
....OK. I have a car seat in my closet.

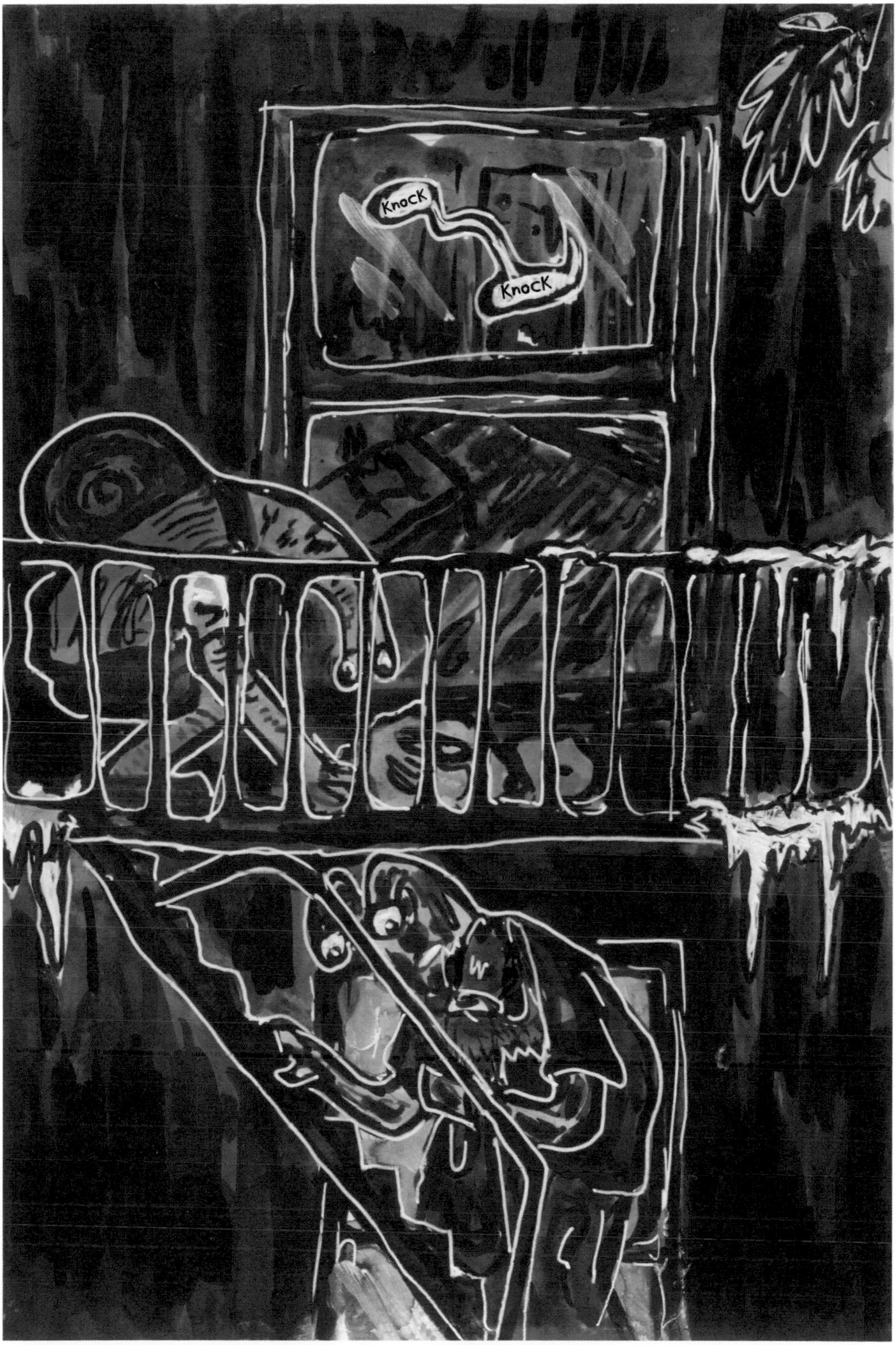
Knock
Knock

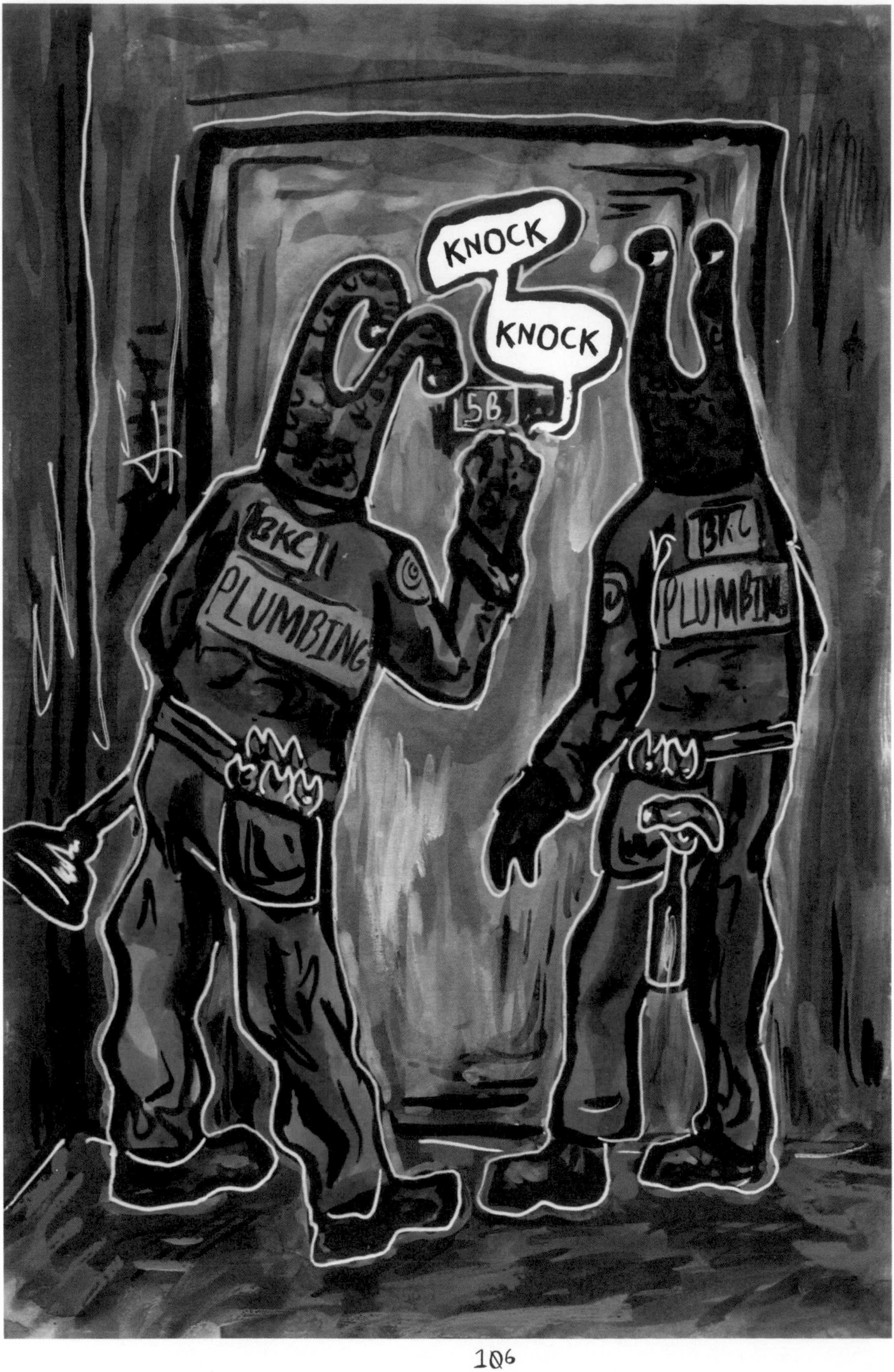
KNOCK
KNOCK
5B
BKC
PLUMBING
BKC
PLUMBING

CHAPTER
6

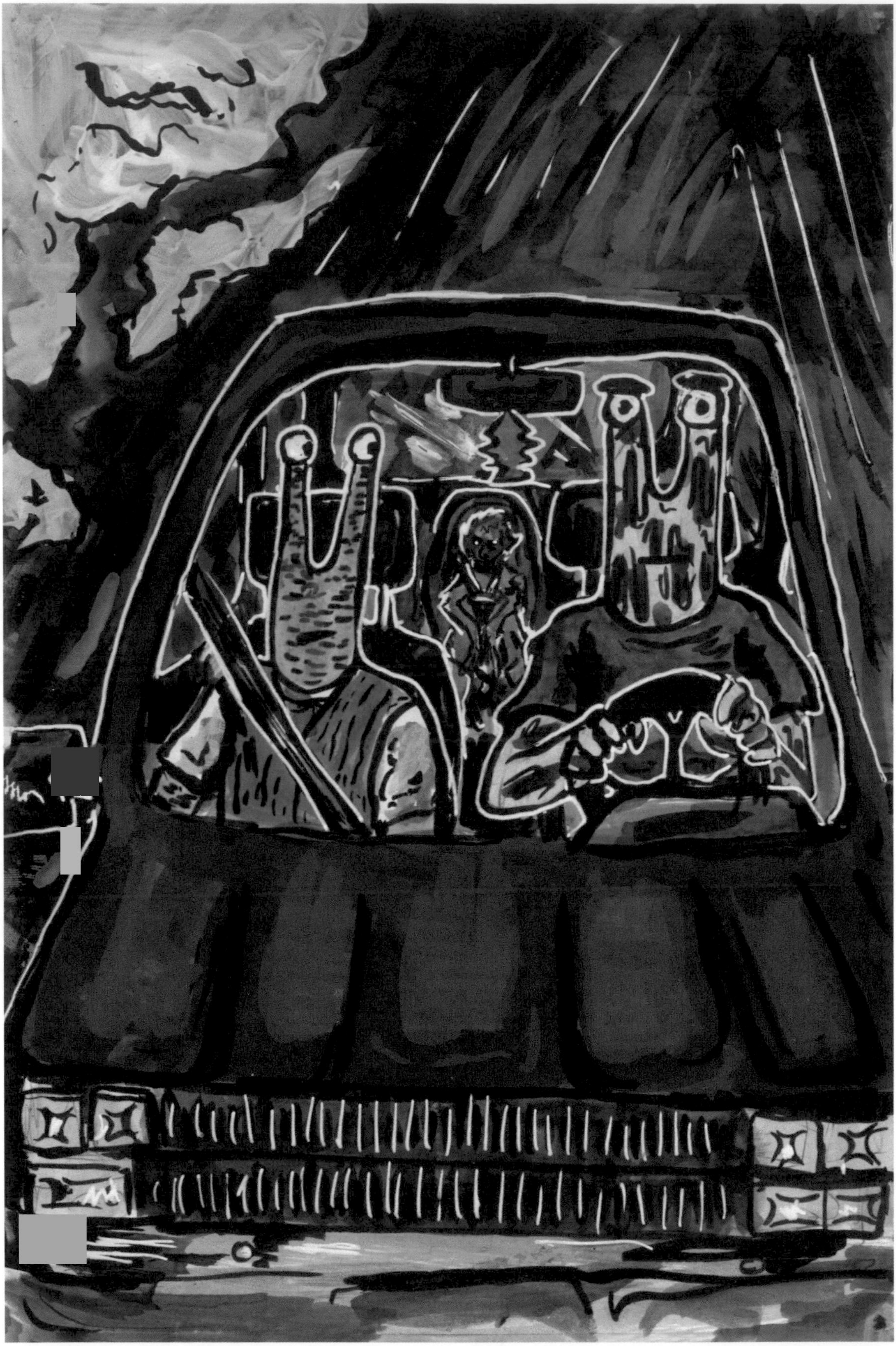

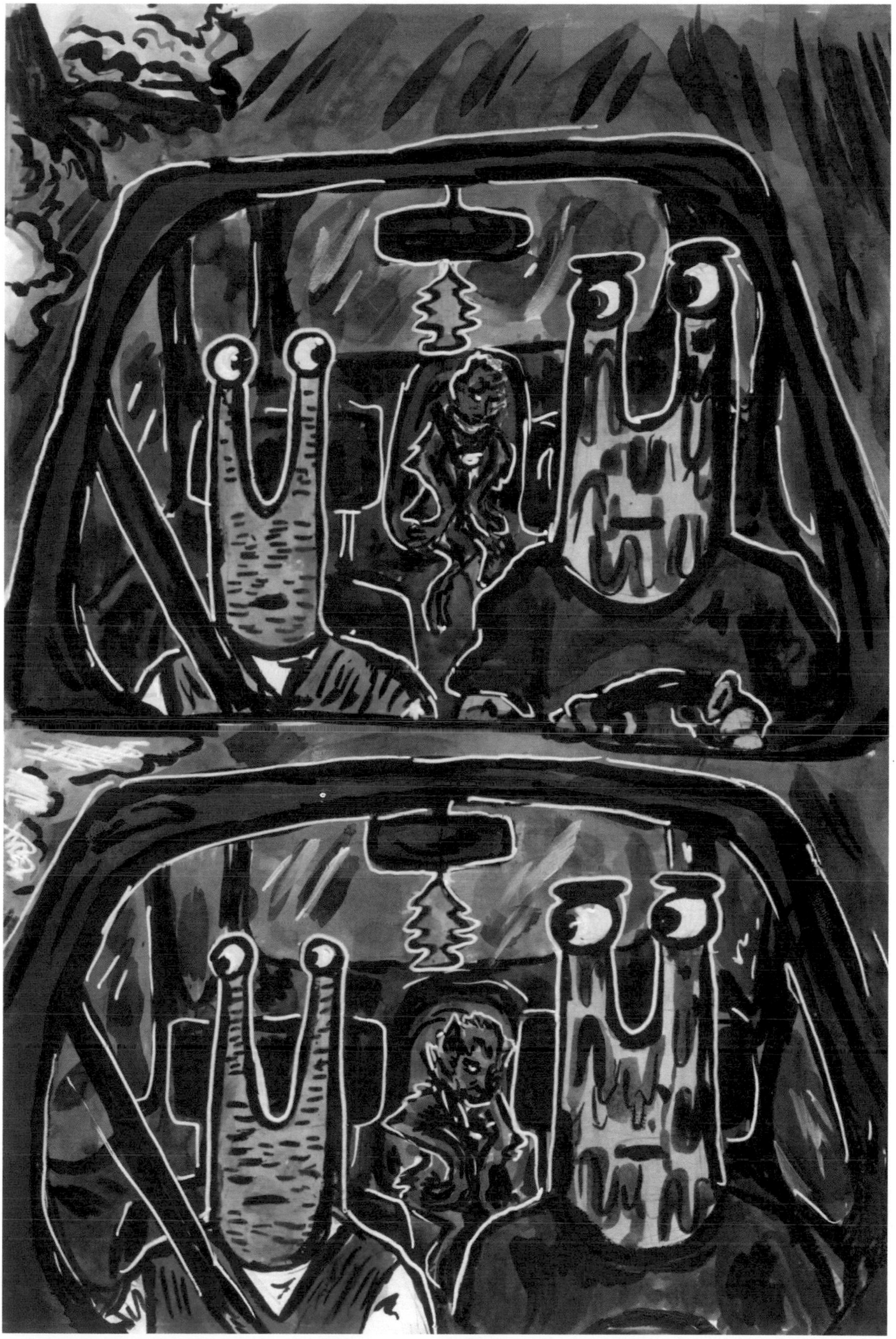

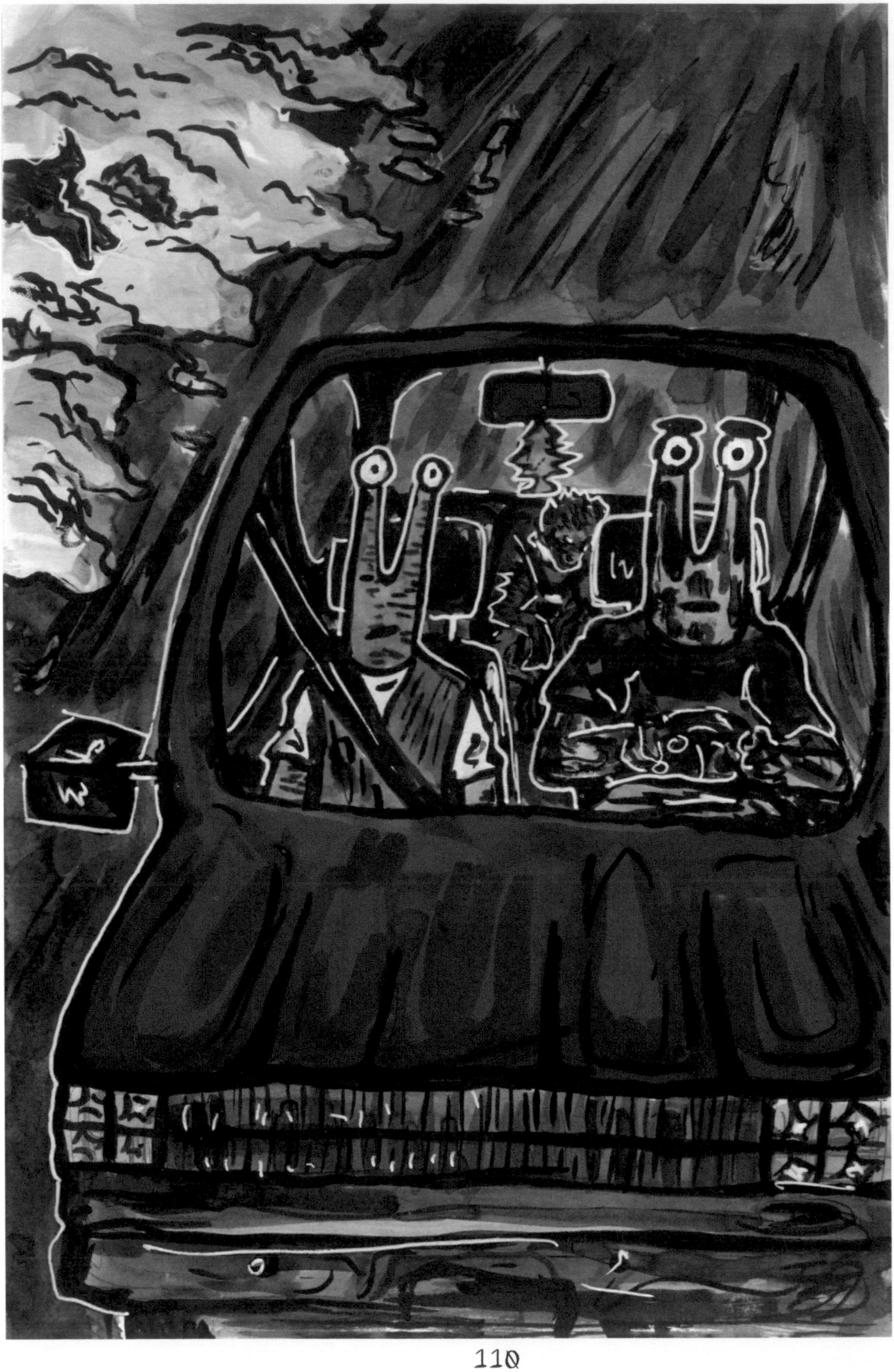

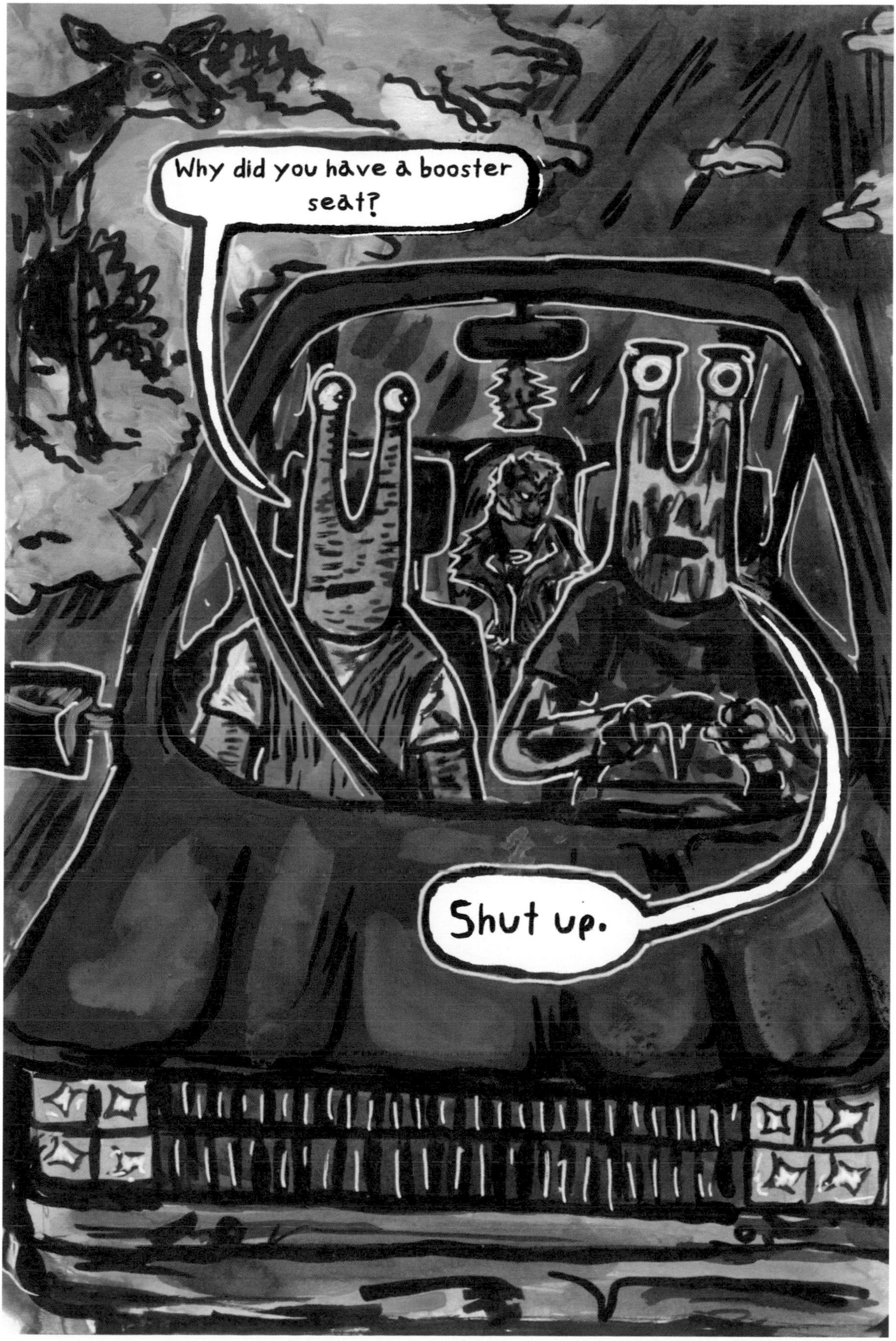
Why did you have a booster seat?
Shut up.

Afterword

Ashley Capps

There's no cathartic resolution to the story of *SALT* a grippingly illustrated graphic novel whose title is doubly resonant for its protagonist, a compassionate gastropod called Silas who is a devoted and exhausted animal liberation activist. Tasked with caring for a mutilated monkey rescued from an obscene vivisection experiment, Silas's hyperawareness of the needless suffering and injustice humans inflict on nonhuman animals is not only a moral compass, but also an existential menace, figurative salt in the wound of existence that threatens to wither the very soul of the sensitive snail as surely as literal salt would disintegrate his body.

In feverish, fervent illustrations, moments of profound tenderness and caregiving are often subsumed in chaotic strokes and claustrophobic intrusions of color and gesture, "tremors of trauma" and psychic turmoil reverberating in every scene. Through these depictions, we vividly glimpse a nervous system on the verge of breakdown, and experience how loudly alone the life of an animal activist can feel, steeped in excruciating witness of atrocities so abject and perverse, the knowledge of their unrelenting dailiness defies sanity. It is a gaslit existence, in which moral wakefulness constantly threatens to transmute from a source of propulsion to poisoned paralysis.

No easy answers or endings emerge. Rather, we are left with a deep sense of disquiet, stirred to reflect on the systems and victims of oppression and supremacy we live amongst, and to interrogate the methods as well as the limits of our resistance. In the omnicidal throes of "gore capitalism" (Sayak Valencia), churning out victims on such a statistically massive scale, questions about the nature of rescue emerge as equally urgent considerations alongside any impulse toward the rescue of nature, including, in this instance, its most denatured, disavowed members, whose hidden plight is searingly and unforgettably brought to light by artist Coyote Jacobs.

Ashley Capps is the Director of Research & Communications at A Well-Fed World, an international hunger relief and food security organization advancing plant-based foods and farming to create a sustainable, nourished, and climate-friendly future. She is also a writer and editor at Free from Harm, a non-profit organization dedicated to helping build a nonviolent mass movement for all species liberation.

About the Author

Coyote Jacobs was born as a large insect under a rock but through a series of increasingly unfortunate events now has to live life as a human man. He forgets when he became an artist but it's the main thing he does. His work draws primarily from his experiences with non-human animals, specifically those rescued from slaughterhouses and other places of exploitation. Within his work, he hopes to create uneasiness with the assumed entitlement over animal lives. He fosters bunny rabbits and is friends with many chickens.

About the Publisher

Lantern Publishing & Media was founded in 2020 to follow and expand on the legacy of Lantern Books—a publishing company started in 1999 on the principles of living with a greater depth and commitment to the preservation of the natural world. Like its predecessor, Lantern Publishing & Media produces books on animal advocacy, veganism, religion, social justice, humane education, psychology, family therapy, and recovery. Lantern is dedicated to printing in the United States on recycled paper and saving resources in our day-to-day operations. Our titles are also available as ebooks and audiobooks.

To catch up on Lantern's publishing program, visit us at www.lanternpm.org.

 facebook.com/lanternpm
instagram.com/lanternpm
twitter.com/lanternpm

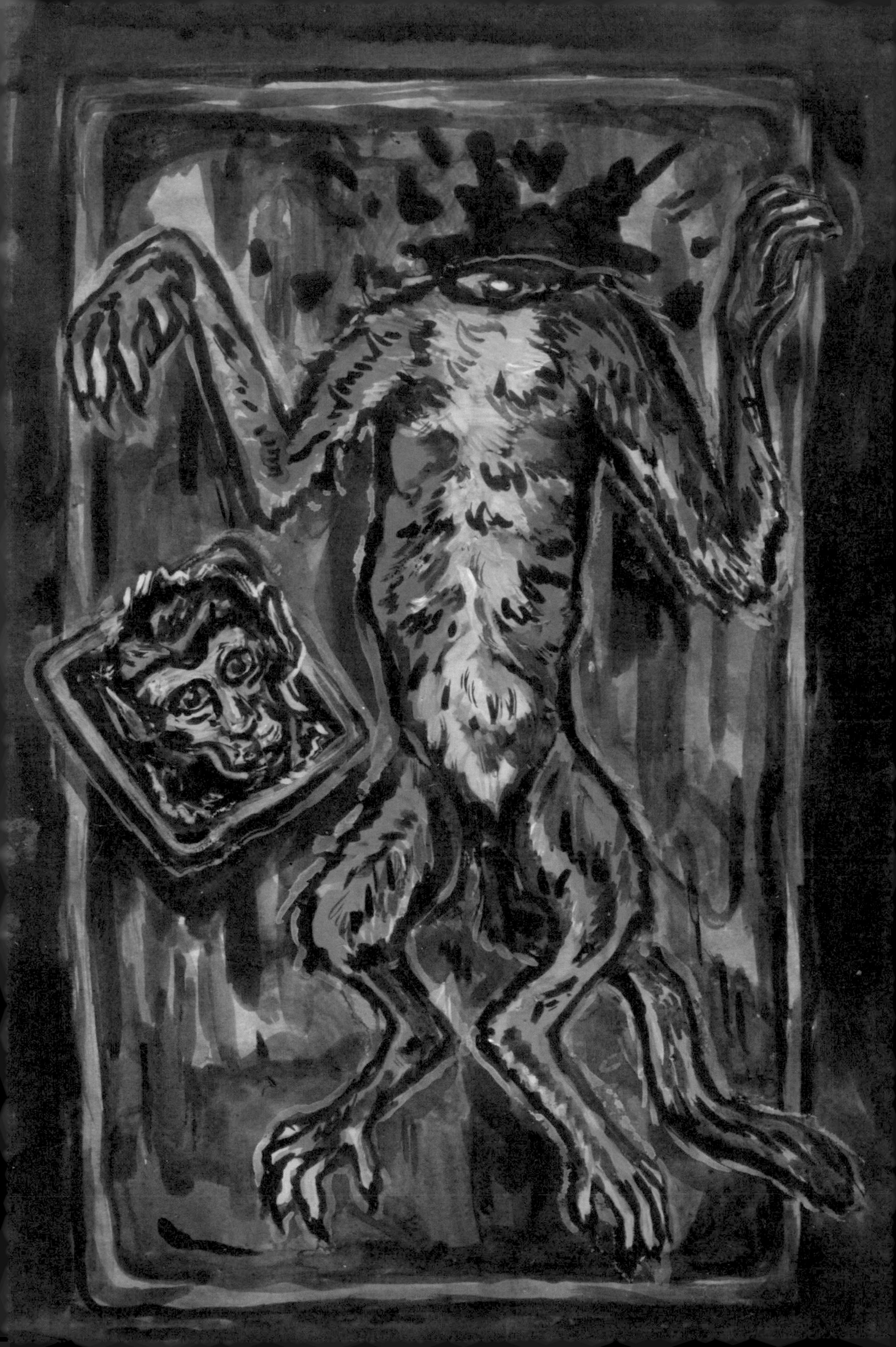

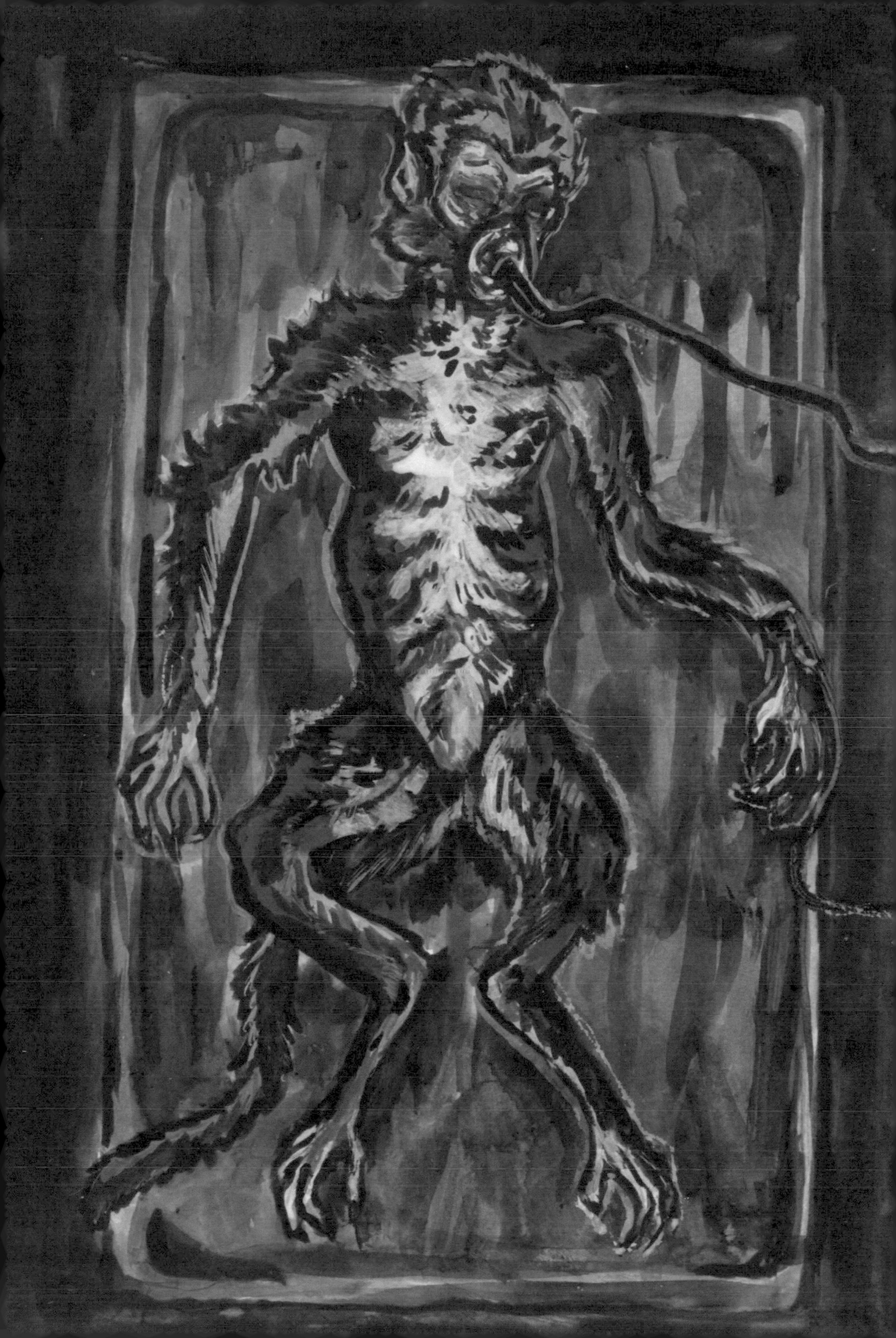